The Sam Sharp

The Sam Sharpe Lectures

2012–22

History, Rebellion and Reform

Dr E. P. Louis
and
Rosemarie Davidson

scm press

British Library Cataloguing in Publication data

A catalogue record for this book is available
from the British Library

ISBN 978-0-334-06547-0

Typeset by Regent Typesetting
Printed and bound in Great Britain by
CPI Group (UK) Ltd

Contents

Foreword

Rosemarie Davidson

The energy and enthusiasm were high at the close of the 2010 Sam Sharpe conference, held at Regent's Park College, Oxford, on the week of 13 April. The theme of the conference was 'Sam Sharpe and the Quest for Liberation: Context, Theology and Legacy for Today'. It was organized by Revd Dr Delroy Reid Salmon and Dr Nick Wood in partnership with the Jamaica Baptist Union (JBU), BMS World Mission (BMS) and Baptists Together (BT). Soon the question of how to continue the dynamic legacy of this beloved Jamaican national hero manifested among the diasporan peoples in the UK. In collaboration with members of the Jamaica Baptist Union, represented by Revd Karl Johnson as General Secretary, two interlinked but separate strands emerged.

First was to create a space to continue and develop themes raised during the conference, which became the Sam Sharpe Project for Research, Education and Community Engagement in partnership with JBU, BMS and BT. The second, the Sam Sharpe Lectures, was proposed by myself as a faith-based but not a faith-specific platform for our thinkers and activists within the African-Caribbean diaspora. It would be a vehicle for the promotion of the pieces of work developed by the educators and theologians associated with the Sam Sharpe Project and keep the name of the project on the radar for the communities we wanted to engage.

My dreams for the Sam Sharpe Lectures were, and remain, lofty: that one day the annual lectures will be on a par with the beloved Reith Lectures hosted by the BBC – internationally renowned with popular appeal. In the formative years of the Sam Sharpe Lectures, there was not a hint that they would last a decade. Lectures take planning, finance and, in our case, much goodwill – often above and beyond. We benefited from the numerous networks and persuasive encouragement and leadership of Revd Wale Hudson-Roberts; the generous support of the officers and staff of the Jamaican High Commission over consecutive administrations; the communication and administrative skills of the Faith and Society Team at Baptists Together, particularly Mary Parker and Revd Mike Lowe; the hospitality of Baptist churches and other denominations across the country; the consistency of the Sam Sharpe Project partners, to say nothing of the faithful and tenacious support of the ever-wise and resourceful Revd Karl Johnson (former General Secretary of the Jamaica Baptist Union, now Senior Pastor of the historic Phillippo Baptist Church in Spanish Town, St Catherine, Jamaica).

Over the past decade, attendees of the Sam Sharpe Lectures have been informed, challenged, enlightened and stirred up. Discussions about each lecture have continued long after the chairs have been cleared, canapés consumed and internet links closed. Each lecture has been as unique as the last. Each facet catches the light of thought, prompting dynamic questions fielded by equally thoughtful and dynamic facilitators from various disciplines.

All but a couple of the lectures are captured in this book. They examine various themes, such as what it means to be a hero (Professor Robert Beckford), righteous rebellion (Revd Dr Joel Edwards CBE), integrity in organizational partnerships seeking justice and reparations (Revd Karl Johnson), the forgotten women in the battle for emancipation (Professor Verene Shepherd) to name a few. Those of us in the room, and those who watched online, will not soon forget the electricity of the moment. We hope that you will be inspired and challenged by reading all the contributions.

Due to circumstances beyond our control, we have not been able to reproduce the lectures of the Rt Revd Bishop Rose Hudson-Wilkin of Dover in the Diocese of Canterbury and Revd Dr Delroy Reid-Salmon of New York, USA. Their contrasting lectures were thought-provoking, and we are honoured that they took the time to participate in the Sam Sharpe Lectures during their fledgling years. Thank you.

As we look to the future, the next ten years and beyond, it is our intention that we also create a platform for the under-25s by the under-25s called Sharpe Young Things. Our youth and young people are not our future – they are our today. So it is important to hear their vision for tomorrow and the inspirations they will draw on to build it.

I am certain that when Sam Sharpe, a young man, stepped up to the gallows in May 1832 for his leadership of the Baptist Rebellion, he did not imagine that today we would still be drawing inspiration from his vision for all men and women before God. He has inspired art, poetry and academia. What will this enslaved person, who taught himself to read and altered the future of his country, inspire in you?

Bringing Down the House

Professor Kehinde Andrews, 2022

It's good to be here. This was a really important invitation because I don't really hear Sam Sharpe's name used at all, which is interesting given there is a big Jamaican population in the UK, and that we do talk about slavery regularly. And one of the things that really always gets to me when we think about slavery is that there's this idea that to talk about slavery is to talk negatively about our people. I've never understood slavery that way. I was taught very differently. I was taught about Sam Sharpe and the Baptist War. I was taught about Nanny of the Maroons. I was taught about Paul Bogle in the afterlife of slavery. I learnt slavery through resistance, so I've never heard this 'If you learn about slavery, it gives you negative feelings'. Never, never something that's ever crossed my mind. And so, Sam Sharpe is somebody certainly we should be much more knowledgeable about, and I'm going to use Sam Sharpe's position to talk through and think about how we understand racism, how we understand Blackness, how we go forward.

I called this talk 'Bringing Down the House'. I'm actually thinking about Robert (Beckford). I remember one of Robert's talks a long time ago called 'House Negro with the Field Negro Mentality'. And I really like that, and I come back to it a lot because this idea of the house and the field is massively important, conceptually, to how we understand race, racism, Blackness in particular, and resistance.

My absolute favourite person in history is Malcolm X. People like Malcolm X are really important. And I'm also really happy to start with Malcolm X in Oxford because, typically, when we think about intellectual labour, we don't think about people like Malcolm X, do we? And for Black people in particular, when we think about our intellectual heritage, it is only recently that there have been any of us in universities. Tonight, there are four Black professors in the room. Only 150 Black professors are in the entire country out of 20,000, and that is an improvement; that is better than it was two years ago. It is only really recently that there has been a critical mass of Black scholars in universities. Most of our intellectual labour has had to be done outside. Think about someone like Queen Nanny of the Maroons. Think about Malcolm X, Claudia Jones, Amy J. and Marcus Garvey. Those are the revolutionary movements on the continent, Kwame Nkrumah, to name a few. If I was going to list my intellectual tradition, very little of it is academic. So, Malcolm, for me, is the most important intellectual of the twentieth century, full stop. Certainly, if we are talking about race and if we are talking about Blackness, there is definitely nobody better to go to than Malcolm. And if you want, the best place to understand race relations, that would be in Malcolm's 1964 speech 'The Ballot or the Bullet'.[1] I recommend you listen to it. You *can* read it – that is the thing about university, they like written stuff – but the oral tradition is really important. Listen to Malcolm's speech – don't read it – *listen*, because listening to it has a different texture; that extra bit is really important, and funny as well.

The concept that underpins this whole talk here is house negro and field negro. One of the other reasons I like Malcolm is because he is unapologetic. A regular on British TV, Calvin Robinson is a right-wing Black commentator. He has a big Afro and is like six foot four; he's massive when you see him – huge guy! Robinson is essentially on TV to say the things white people can't say: racism doesn't exist, Black Lives Matter is a joke, and so on. I have spent far too much time on TV with people like Calvin Robinson. We were having a debate, and somebody tweeted that people called him a 'house negro', and this comment got lots of complaints; it was in the newspaper. They even starred out the word 'negro' – I didn't realize negro was a swear word. These kinds of terms – house negro – have become a racial slur. But no, 'house negro' and 'field negro' is intellectual labour, Black intellectual labour.

The whole point of house negro/field negro is articulated by Malcolm in the speech 'Message to the Grassroots',[2] which, again, you have to listen to – you can't read that speech, you have to listen to it, listen to the intonation, the tone, the pauses, the jokes. It's a very funny speech. He's using this plantation story, the metaphor of the slave plantation, and saying you have the house and the field. In the house, the conditions are slightly better. From what? You're still a slave, and it's really important to remember this – a house negro is still a slave; they're not saved from slavery. They are just in the house. They don't have the worst labour. They're closer to the house, they get treated slightly better, but they are still slaves. They still get beaten, they still get raped and they're still property. What he's arguing is that because you're in the house, you have more proximity to the master and slightly better conditions. It's easy to get confused and think that you're doing better. That you don't need to bring down the house; you don't need to run away because, actually, the house is all right. And in the speech he comments that the house negro says, 'Where can I get a better house than this? Where can I get better clothes? There's nothing better than this. This is the lot.' And he uses that as a metaphor for a lot of Black middle-class people in America – and you could say in Britain today. There is no doubt all of us professors are in the material position of being house negroes. I get paid very well – I'm all right – I really don't get most of the problems of racism. I still get quite a bit of it, but not all of it, you know. We still get racism, but it will be easy for someone in my position to be confused and think that it's OK. That things aren't that bad, and it's getting better – that we are moving on – although, actually, as a Black professor, that is pretty much impossible because you get reminded every day that racism is a real thing. But generally, that's the basic notion. People get carried away and believe that things are progressing all right.

Malcolm contrasts that with the field negro. The field negro is that person who's in the field, sun up to sundown, getting whipped, getting the lash. In that position, there's no way you could possibly think that slavery was anything other than an abomination that needed to be destroyed. And so, what you're saying is these are two different positions: one is authentic and one is inauthentic. The house negro is in an inauthentic position because it's not true. You're deluded. You think something is OK. You're thinking that Britain is going to end racism. But does anybody actually think that? Does anybody actually think that racism in Britain will end anytime soon? Nobody thinks it. I'll come back to that because it's quite an important point, but the house negro is inauthentic because of that.

We think about authenticity often because when we have this Black authenticity discussion, house negro becomes related to middle-class people who talk properly, have white friends and have white partners. But that's not what Malcolm is saying. What he's saying is that it is the belief in the system that is oppressing you, which makes your mentality inauthentic. This is why I like that Robert talks about the 'house negro with a field negro mentality'. You can be in the house and have a field negro mentality. You can understand that the system is fundamentally racist and needs to be overturned. It's more of a mentality than it is a class thing.

So, we're thinking about the house – I'm bringing down the house – this is why I like Sam Sharpe. Sam Sharpe is on the plantation, he's enslaved, but he's not saying, 'How do I reform slavery?' He's not saying, 'How do we make the working conditions on the plantation slightly better?' No, he's saying we need to end it; we need to burn it and then get rid of it; we need to bring the thing collapsing down. And it's that revolutionary spirit. I don't say we lack it completely, but we do kind of because, in Malcolm's time, you don't have race relations legislation in America; you don't have race relations legislation here. You probably don't have in the UK four Black professors *full stop*. It was a very different place, where we actually weren't really *in* the society in any real way. Think about the Universal Negro Improvement Association, the largest Black organization in history. We had between two and eight million members across 50 countries. That was the 1920s because, in the 1920s, no Black person thought that there was anything you could get from America, the Caribbean or Britain. Everybody understood that this was a plantation. And we have to resist. What's the big change that has happened over the last 50 years? It is that we now have some access. We have more Black professors, and we have an over-representation of Black students at universities. Not an over-representation at universities like this one in Oxford, but at universities like mine, Birmingham City University. So, it's not perfect, but there's an over-representation of Black students at university. You have Black middle-class people. We could almost have had – and might still have – a Black prime minister!

So that's what's changed. What's changed now is that, in a very real way, all of us are now in the house. We have some protection under the law. You're in the welfare state. Believing in the UK means that even if you're Black, you're still one of the top 80 per cent earners in the entire world. That's the reality. So, it has opened up enough, and we're kind of all in the house. And so now we're all thinking, 'Can we fix Britain? Can we just try and make it better? Can we?' Just trying to improve the law that we have on the plantation rather than thinking this is the plantation, and there is no way to reform it. The only thing you can do is to bring it down. This is why I write radically; my work is radicalism. But I would stress it is very difficult to maintain that position as a professor because the professor is firmly in the house. So, this whole talk really is my existential crisis about how to do Black radical work in the house – properly, firmly ensconced in there. And it might be that by the end of the talk I convince myself that I need to resign, and then there are only three Black professors. I don't know.

The Haitian Revolution – a Model

I'm going to start here because this ties into Sam Sharpe and our thinking about rebellion. And very much this is the field. There is a picture called *Bwa Kayiman*.[3] It depicts the start of the Haitian Revolution in 1791. I start here because, again, this is how I learned about slavery. I didn't learn about it negatively;

I learned about it positively. In fact, from that perspective, there is not really much negative at all; slavery is about resistance, it's about survival, and it is about lots of other things. So, Haiti, 1791 – this is a Vodon ceremony led by Boukman Dutty, who was originally enslaved in Jamaica and then was sold to Haiti, and Cecile Fatima, who was a practitioner of Vodon. This image and event say important things about the theological context as well. This is one of the arguments as to why Haiti is the only successful slave rebellion in recorded history, because roughly 60 per cent of the enslaved in Haiti were born in Africa, not born in Haiti. French slavery was such that they essentially worked the slaves to death. The average life expectancy was less than 40 years. So, they just worked you to death and then brought in new people, like a conveyor belt. This meant that about 60 per cent of the enslaved were from Africa and that in turn meant they also had their indigenous tongues, indigenous skills and indigenous religion.

One of the unfortunate contexts of Christianity is that it was used to pacify Black people in Africa and in the Caribbean. But there was a seasoning process, a breaking-in process for people taken from Africa, which was to remove languages, tongues, names, religions, and install a particular version – and I say a *particular* version – of Christianity, which would pacify them. One of the explanations for why it happened was because you've got 60 per cent of people who have refused to be broken in. There was also a civil war happening in the region of the Congo, so a lot of people were sold after being captured and were actually warriors. This meant that they had lots of skills in warfare. They seem to be very African, very traditional and very connected to their beliefs. Thus the Haitian Revolution was successful by 1804.

It's not a coincidence that the British government abolished the slave trade in 1807. And I stress the slave *trade*. Slavery continued in the British Empire until the 1830s. From 1834, there was a four-year period of apprenticeship. Because apparently we did not know how to be free, so we needed to learn how to be free for four years. Apprenticeship was spending 75 per cent of our time working for free on plantations. So, slavery did not end in the Caribbean until 1838. If anybody tells you it was in 1834, that is not true – it was 1838. In fact, Sir Professor Hilary Beckles did a lot of work on reparations in the Caribbean. The University of the West Indies says that the Abolition Act (An Act for the Abolition of the Slave Trade) was the most racist piece of legislation ever passed by the British government. This is for two reasons: first, it is an apprenticeship. We do not know how to be free, and therefore we have to work 75 per cent of our time for four years. And second, it is the biggest payment ever made by the government to any entity for anything, which is the slave-owner compensation, which was £20 million at the time, often quoted as being £17 billion today. That is a massive underestimate. It was 5 per cent of the GDP. That's £100 billion in today's money, 40 per cent of the government's entire budget that year. The money they paid to slave owners to abolish slavery was unprecedented. The government had taken a colossal loan – and when did they actually pay it back? In 2015, right? 2015. So everybody in this room, all of you, you might be proud to learn that you paid back slave-owner compensation through your taxes. Just makes you feel happy. You abolished slavery. Well done. My grandmother was not happy to learn that she and her mother and those whom she was descended from (the enslaved) were paying back slave-owner compensation, but there you go.

So it was the most racist legislation. The reason I bring this up is that in 1807 Britain abolished the slave trade. This was not a moral act. Slavery continued for 31 entire years.

The motivation for abolishing the slave trade was twofold. One was because French slavery needed new Africans. Britain had a different model where they had more people born into slavery, and Britain basically didn't need it; they didn't need slavery any more; they just bred slaves. And if we can stop the trade in France, who is the direct competitor, their colonies will go down. It was William Pitt Jr who learned that 50 per cent of the enslaved who were on British slave ships were for the French plantation. He said, 'What are we doing? Why are we supporting French slavery? Let's abolish the slave trade; then French slavery can't happen, and we will be dominant.' It was all about economics. And the second reason is that they were terrified of Africans. We need to stop bringing Africans in with their religion, African religion, African traditions and African craft. Britain basically calculated that they had enough people, they could keep breeding, and keep slavery going on for a long time without the slave trade. It was not a moral reason. And so, when people tell you that the British navy went around freeing slaves and destroying slave ships, that wasn't because they were against slavery, it was because they didn't want the competition. Simple as that. There's a great book by Stella Dadzie called *A Kick in the Belly*,[4] which shows that again, thinking about agency, the Haitian Revolution is the best example of agency by Black people. We just ended the thing. And the first country to abolish slavery was not Britain; it was Haitians in 1804 that abolished it themselves.

So, Britain makes this calculation that we can keep slavery going through breeding. After the abolition of the slave trade, the birth rate in the Caribbean plummets, and it only comes back up after slavery has been abolished. And the only explanation for this? Could it be that the enslaved women knew what the masters were doing and said, 'We're not going to breed the next generation of the enslaved', hence slavery becomes abolished in the 1830s? People often say it was economical, but the economics stop working because the slaves stopped having children – there were not enough slaves to carry on.

The second reason slavery was abolished in 1833/34 is the Baptist War in 1831. Again, these aren't coincidences. They have 20,000 Africans led by Sam Sharpe, who said, 'No, we're not doing this, bun it',[5] and they get terrified, and so slavery becomes abolished. In all of these parts, we are active agents in this history. Sam Sharpe is a perfect example of that. There are lots of examples of it. The other reason I bring this out is the idea of the field – the grass roots. Where do we get our knowledge from? This, to me, is knowledge. The Haitian Revolution is knowledge. In fact, if you want to read a book that will tell you so much about problems, negotiations and how you do Black politics, C. L. R. James's *The Black Jacobins* is perfect.[6] Why does the Haitian Revolution take from 1791 to 1804?

The main reason is massive division. At this point, the people who are burning the plantations are the field negroes. It's the grass roots who are saying, 'We are done, but we are not having this.' In Haitian society, you had the enslaved and a class of what they call mulatto, which is a terrible word that we should never use, installed in a buffer zone. Some of the privileged were not enslaved and managed a lot of the island. And there were also free Blacks. In fact, Toussaint Louverture, whom you may have heard of, was free and was really important later on in the Haitian Revolution. He also had slaves as well. That should tell you something about how the politics worked on the island. Toussaint and the mulattos weren't involved. At this point, the field negro was burning so much that almost everybody had to get involved. So *The Black Jacobins* is perfect because it really speaks to all these discussions and negotiations; how does everybody get involved? The mixed-race class and the free Blacks don't get involved until they have to get involved. Until they just go with the popular choice, 'You are either with us, or you're against us.' And they got with us (the Haitian slaves). We see that knowledge is driven from the grass roots. The authentic position is the field negro, but that doesn't mean everybody can't join that position.

Haiti is a really good starting point and a really good example of lots of things. The first country to abolish slavery was Haiti. We do Black studies at the university, and I always say this to people, and even to students: the first year is the canon and the body of literature for Black studies isn't academic. The root of Black studies isn't academic at all. It is Haiti. It is resistance. It is Sam Sharpe.

Black Studies is Grass Roots

I have a lot of books in my house. Mostly, I just stole them from my parents' house. I was fortunate, and this is why. If I took what is my intellectual tradition and heritage, why do I not necessarily have the same understanding of what it is to be an intellectual as many academic colleagues? It is because this was

my upbringing. There was British Black Power. I was very fortunate. Most people don't have it operating in their houses. One
of the things I always stress about Black Power is that its main
contribution was education. Think about the 1960s: my mum
and dad were growing up in the '60s and '70s; you couldn't just
go on Amazon – I've named you four books, you can buy them,
they'll be in your house tomorrow. That was not the case in the
1960s. You couldn't get these books. So, one of the things you
had in the Black movement was a bookshop movement. There
were Saturday schools, community organization meetings and
bookshops.

My dad would tell stories about going to Los Angeles to go
to some guy's house in the hood, up ten flights of stairs to get
this one book and bring it back into the country. That's what
it was like back in the day. Now we are totally spoiled with the
knowledge that we can get. In the '60s and '70s, they are building a canon, which includes Garvey and the Black Panthers.
One of the things I have noticed now is that it doesn't include
many women; it is a very male-centred canon. That is changing.
I always stress that Black studies is new in the *university*. But
it's not new elsewhere. We didn't come from nowhere; we came
from a very, very, very long tradition of Black studies, which
we have now brought into the university. And it doesn't always
work; there are always problems.

If you think about what the British Black Panthers did, it
was largely educational. It was what we call Saturday school,
which was organized in the community. It was events, it was
protest, it was speakers. This is one of the really underrated
things historically in the UK: because the UK is the centre of
empire, it means that pretty much everybody has come through
Britain at some point. The Panthers, Stokely Carmichael (or
Kwame Ture) came here in 1968. And they speak and really
inspire lots of people; Malcolm came over, then Martin (Luther
King Jr) came. Everybody came from the States but also from
African countries. In fact, my dad left community organization
in the late 1970s, and the reason he gives is that he was sharing a platform with a revolutionary leader in Zimbabwe; they
were talking, and sharing this platform, and in the next week

the revolutionary leader was assassinated, and he was, like, 'I'm not really serious, this guy is serious!', maybe I need to rethink, and so he became a lawyer and did criminal defence work. These events, these days, are very difficult to appreciate now because we have so much access to information. The book *Stokely Speaks*[7] was very, very important in my own personal journey. For my 16-year-old self, reading this completely transformed the way I felt about things. This kind of educational journey is really, really important – you don't get this education in school, and you won't get this education in the media. But Black communities historically have been very good, having to make sure that we get the education elsewhere, and we definitely need to continue; otherwise, we will be lost, believe me.

Resisting Racism: Race, Inequality, and the Black Supplementary School Movement[8] is a book I've written based on a 50-year tradition of Black communities basically saying racism is terrible, so we're going to organize our own schools, teach ourselves. Self-help is a whole movement in the UK, from schools to housing, employment agencies and legal defence – self-help. This is something I would say we've lost as a community; it's the question of 'Why are you relying on the state for anything?' We know the state is racist, and you should definitely notice racism now; if you don't know now, then you're never going to know. So we have to do our own thing, build our own stuff. And this is what Saturday schools are. We say, 'Look – there are things the schools won't teach, so we'll teach.' Saturday schools are different because most ethnic minority groups have some kind of supplementary education, but it's usually about culture or religion or language. These are things you wouldn't expect to be taught in school. Saturday schools were primarily about maths and English. The kids were coming out unable to read; that's how bad it was in the 1960s. Lots of them don't have any Black stories to them at all, they are just about maths and English. But then you also have this movement that said, 'Look, we need Black studies, we need to think, we need to engage differently, we need to create a different canon, a different curriculum.' This was at least a 50-year history, but there was a lack of understanding of the history. So, as I always say, I'm not a historian, but if you do this work, you have to be a historian. So actually, when I did *Saturday Schools*, I wasn't writing from a historical perspective at all. But then when I went to write a book, there was no book about Saturday schools. So, I had to write a book. One of the projects we're currently trying to get money for is around the oral history of 200 Black Power activists in the '60s and '70s, because it's really poorly understood and there is a lack of documentation. If we don't interview the people soon, then it dies, it literally disappears.

Vanley Burke, who is a historian of Black people generally, Birmingham in particular, and Handsworth specifically, took a picture of great significance at African Liberation Day 1977 in Handsworth Park, Birmingham.[9] It was the first Africa Liberation Day in Birmingham, the third in the UK, and again this is an idea that was there with these spaces and education, where you can learn different things, gain understanding and bring together the community in a very different way. That's why I said Black studies is not new at all. This is what I grew up in, and this is the only tradition that I know, a tradition that is rooted in the grass roots, rooted in community and can't exist without community. I use this as an example of something we did eight years ago. The Harambee Organization for Black Unity in Birmingham used to be at the Harriet Tubman Development Centre, which was the Harriet Tubman Book Shop on Grove Lane, and which anybody from Birmingham would probably have been to. It is one of those spaces where we bought in different books, different education. I was volunteered to work there as a young person a number of times by my parents. In 2012, we tried to save that particular building, and for various reasons we could not. But we still do have Lynwood Road, which used to be the Marcus Garvey Nursery, and which is now the Marcus Garvey Centre. There is also Harambee House, which started out as a hostel for Black people. That's just to give you an example of the kind of self-help initiatives that people started – 'The state won't do it, so we will.'

We said, 'Let's do community talks, discussions and events. Let's go out and talk to people, right? That's what we should do.' This is where you get the best kind of knowledge. And the reason I use this particular example is that the major problem with universities, if you can break it down, is simply that they are elite bubbles where you only ever talk to anybody else in the bubble. Basically, the problem is the people – most of the people in the bubble are white and elite.

Paul Gilroy is probably the most esteemed Black intellectual in the UK (esteemed by whom is a good question, but esteemed within the bubble). Gilroy talks and writes in a particular way that only works because of who Gilroy is talking to. His audience is not the community and is not the grass roots at all – it's the people within the bubble. And that's what keeps universities separate and elite. I mean, it is good to see people from the community in the university tonight because think about how many times you ever really go into a university if you don't work there or, now, you're not paying to be there. These are not spaces you can go into, because you have to swipe in. Essentially this is the problem with the university: it is elite and separate.

In order to become professor, I had to write things that I would never write now, because I don't care. I don't have to worry about promotions, or about journal articles that literally suck the life out of you. So, in university, we have something called open access. You actually can't read a lot of the journal articles because you have to pay, there's a paywall. There's a big push to get open access so people can read them. I would say it's pointless. The problem isn't that people can't read them. The problem is, even if you could read them, I guarantee you wouldn't want to read them anyway. We actually have a way of talking, thinking, writing and expressing views that is deeply elitist and separate, and it only makes sense within the bubble. You will find a lot of the people *we* think of as famous nobody knows. Only within the bubble does it make any sense. Outside the bubble, it doesn't make any sense. This is why the idea of the public intellectual, for me, is a really problematic idea. All intellectual work should be public. By its very definition of being an intellectual, you should have to talk and engage with the public. And if you don't, then what are we doing? That's why, for me, why would I not go and talk to the public? The reason I go on about this is that doing it actually makes your work better. If I was going to critique Paul Gilroy's work on Blackness – he writes quite a bit about Blackness – it's bad because he just talks to the bubble. You can't understand Blackness within this place. If you only reference within the university, you're going to misunderstand Blackness. You have to be outside; you have to be talking. That's what makes the work make sense, right?

In 2012 I said, 'Black is a country.' I still say Black is a country. My son looks at me and says, 'Don't be ridiculous, Black isn't a country; there's no passport, there's no border!' I had this experience in Handsworth bookshop doing a talk called 'Black is a Country'. There were 50 people packed into the building talking about 'Black is a country'. This Zimbabwean guy comes in. He's mad, mad, mad, mad (angry). He's like, 'You can't say Black is a country – that is racist. There's so many different countries.' This is the reason to talk. I'm not joking; by the end of the talk, he interrupted me to say, 'Black is a country!' That's the kind of affirmation that's important, not the peer review. Actually, in the process of that discussion, it changed some of the things I was thinking about it, and so *Back to Black*[10] is a book that this is in, and it's academic in some ways and not academic. It's not boring is what I am trying to say. It is essentially a theory book about Black radicalism and Black politics. But I couldn't have done it without this story. I couldn't have done it without ten years of actually doing the work. It wouldn't make any sense. And that's how we have to think about our work. It has to be connected to the grass roots, even though, as I said, I'm very firmly in the house negro position. You have to make an effort to go and make sure you're engaging outside – otherwise, you get lost.

Black Studies is Community

Claudia Jones is an underappreciated figure who was born in Trinidad. She moved to America with her family, was a communist there, and became very high up in the Communist Party. She was deported in the McCarthy trials, but she wasn't deported to Trinidad. Where was she deported, do you think? Even in the Caribbean they did not want her, because in the Caribbean at the time, in particular, there was massive unrest. They said, 'We can't send Claudia Jones to Trinidad; she would be a problem', so they sent her to the UK. Why Britain? That's a bit strange. How could they legally send her to Britain? Trinidad was not a country in 1955; it was part of the British Empire, and her nationality was British, so they could deport her to Britain. This is the thing about Britain, Britain is empire, Britain is not a nation-state. This is why Claudia Jones ends up here, and the logic is that she will be safe in Britain. But no, obviously, she carries on. She carries on organizing, organizing anti-immigration legislation and campaigns, and organizes the first Black British newspaper, the *West Indian Gazette*. She helps organize the things that lead to the Notting Hill Carnival after the 1958 race riot. The race riot – the actual definition is when white people get mad about Black people, and they start burning things. That's a race riot, and the UK has had a number of them, including 1958. After that, Claudia Jones is one of a group that organizes cultural events to, she says, 'wash the taste out of our mouths' of the event, but also to raise money for the legal defence fees of the Black people who got caught up with the police after the riot, and that becomes the Notting Hill Carnival. So, Claudia Jones is a really important figure in the UK. I strongly recommend the book *Claudia Jones: Beyond Containment*,[11] which is a collection of her writings. Again, she is a very under-appreciated academic.

Black studies in the USA is very similar to the UK in the sense that the knowledge of Black studies is outside of the university. What gets Black studies in America is the Black Power movement, and it's not a coincidence. In 1969 there is the first Black studies department in San Francisco State. It is very much Black power. Black Panthers are involved here; without the external politics, there is no Black studies in the United States; it simply doesn't exist. So how do we bring this knowledge into the university and transform the university?

Nathaniel Hare, who's one of the founders of Black studies, talks about the community component being the most important component. I stress that is the most important component because it is the thing that separates the ivory tower elite from Black studies, which is about organically connecting to the community. That's why I always say that Black studies is not African studies, not Caribbean studies; it's not even African American studies. You can do all of those things without the community component. Actually, most of those things, even African American studies, are done without the community component. It is a community component that makes Black studies different because it means it is always organically connected, always rooted.

In the degree, for example, students have to do a placement – that's the language of the university – in a community, either with the community organization or doing stuff in the community. After they apply Black studies, they have to do a Black studies project where they can prove that the project itself wasn't just a research thing for their benefit but actually had a benefit to the communities as well. As a method, we're saying that this is essential to Black studies.

In 1969, Black students in the Afro-American Society basically occupied the Willard Straight Hall, which was like a student centre in the university. They didn't go in armed; they went in unarmed; they had lots of threats from the Ku Klux Klan, so they armed themselves in the building afterwards – there is a picture of them with the negotiators as they walked out. They call this the battle for Black studies in America – it really was like an actual battle. There was a physical threat. In the UK, it hasn't been that at all; it's been far easier than you think. We didn't have to arm ourselves. But it does tell you how dangerous these ideas can be, right? You are trying to do something that really fundamentally goes against the principles of the place itself. In the UK context, things are slightly different. So you have movements like 'Why is my Curriculum White?' pushing this agenda from the student level, and then we have Black studies come in on that wave in some senses as well, but again the reason why it took longer in the UK rather than America is largely demographic; there are fewer Black people here whereas in America there have always been lots of Black people in America. But also, in the UK, widening participation happened later, around 1992.

Even in places like Oxford, it's only been recently that you've had critical masses of Black students, and they come into the place and say, 'What on earth is this?' They say we need change, fundamental overhaul, and reform, which is why that delay – it happened because, in the UK, this whole widening participation happened later. But it's the same kind of context. There are some people coming to the university saying there's something wrong with it. One of those I did mention earlier is the lack of Black women on the book list. And this is the problem historically for many things. But there had been a big push in terms of Black studies; when you look at Black studies now, the biggest part of it is Black feminism. There's lots and lots of work, lots of stuff produced in the USA, people like Kiesha Blain,[12] who has written about Black women in the Garvey movement in the civil rights movement. In the UK, you have people like Stella Dadzie.[13] There is a lot of work on this, and it is a credit to where we're trying to go, right? Because we need to decolonize, it doesn't just mean Black people; it means adding in the things that are missing. And women's voices, feminist voices, queer voices – they're missing. So those things are trying to be done right. There's some good. Development is certainly happening, and Black feminism is one of the key strands in our course as well.

I got my professorship in 2018. I received a letter from the Committee for the Conferment of Academic Titles. I tweeted it, and the students in the class were all celebrating and clapping. This is Black studies – it's critical, and obviously, when you come to Black studies, you spend the first several weeks going, 'Why am I doing this course?' It's very, very critical, and so we actually end up having a three-hour conversation about why you shouldn't be happy that I got made professor of Black studies.

What do you think the people who signed my letter have in common? You know, three white men, which isn't the end of the world. It just tells you something about the power structure of the university in terms of the Committee for the Conferment of Academic Titles. How many Black studies experts do you think they had on that committee? Zero, right? Think about it – you submit an application. 'I've done all these wonderful things. I should be a professor.' But none of the people who decided knew anything about Black studies. Not one of them knew anything. How is this a legitimate title? It's not right, really. I get paid more, it's great. But when we actually look at what this is we see that it is terrible. This is nonsense. This is totally and utterly inauthentic. This is house stuff, right? And worse than that, think about the things I had to do to become a professor – it wasn't the public intellectual stuff, and it wasn't community stuff. It wasn't the activism stuff. I spent a lot of time writing non-academic stuff; it wasn't any of it. I had to produce many peer-reviewed articles, say I've got this much money from these people (in terms of funding), and I've done this many talks within the bubble – what I called the white stuff. That's how I got promoted in this panel of people who know nothing about Black studies. That is why you very rarely hear me say 'professor'. For me, 'professor' is an illegitimate title. It just gives me more money. Nice. Thank you. I appreciate it. But, actually, my favourite response to this was a lot of people saying, 'Oh, we thought you already were a professor.' Bless you. Well, I like that. I take that. I'll take that as a credential.

When you get made professor, your life changes a little bit, financially certainly, but also in terms of invitations that you get. I had a very public fallout at a previous university because, when we were there, they closed down our sociology department and fired all the Black members. I'm not joking; it happened in 2011. We had a big public 'Save our Sociology' campaign on local TV. They hated me when I left the university. Honestly, they hated me. In fact, I went for a job a while ago and the head dean was the dean of the previous university. There was a two-part interview. One was the department that said I got all the way, that, yeah, 'We love you!' The Dean wouldn't even meet me for the second part of the interview. All of a sudden, I wasn't in this process any more. That's how much they don't like me. But after I got my professorship, I got an invitation from the Vice Chancellor of the University of Birmingham. Who I know knows me. Who I know doesn't like me. We publicly fell out. So, I get an invitation for dinner at his house. I literally spoke with my wife for about three hours – should I accept the invitation? I was terrified; you don't know these people. I don't know, right? Anyway, I'm half joking but not really. The worst part of this story isn't that I actually went. I went there; we sat around; there were other Black academics from the university (it was Black History Month, after all). But the worst part is – it was all right.

We sat there and chatted (other than the servings of food, which were really small. I don't know. We had like six courses, and I still had to go to KFC afterwards). It was quite fun, and that told me that a process is already happening. Ten years before this, if I had got an invitation, there's no chance that I would have gone, or I'd have thrown paint all over the place. So, something's obviously changed in ten years for me to sit there and laugh at the jokes, right? I have already changed. That's what being in the house does to you. It changes you. And this is why I talk about doing the white stuff because I had to spend a lot of time doing that stuff, and it's not like a little thing; it takes so long to do it. So, I've already been changed by the process of being in the house. And this is the danger. This is why I will try to be negative about everything. You get some perspective. And I've seen it in lots of colleagues, in the way that you have to adapt to fit. You could say the same thing about the church or any other institution. People tend to become the institution. You don't change institutions as much as you like to think. That is why I always say for Black studies, we're not trying to decolonize university; we're trying to colonize university. You can't decolonize this thing, but you can use some of the influence from it.

Sam Sharpe, the Slave Preacher

This is where I get to Sam Sharpe. A slave preacher is the only way I can think about being a Black studies professor with radical ideas in the university. The professor is essentially like a slave preacher. It sounds negative but, believe me, it's going to be positive towards the end. So, what was the role? It was to teach a very passive version of Christianity that would make people feel enslaved, keep them enslaved, happy singing and dancing, and teach them that the work for the slave master was the purpose of Christianity; that was the purpose of the slave preacher. And many people did that – they went around, they talked – but is it a coincidence that Sam Sharpe ... what was he? A slave preacher! Nat Turner? Slave preacher. Denmark Vesey? Slave preacher. Look at lots of the rebellions on plantations – they were slave preachers. Because they were slave preachers, they had particular advantages other people didn't have. So, for example, you could not gather in large numbers in any circumstance other than slave preaching, right? The congregations gather. Lots of people meet together. You couldn't read; you were banned from reading other than reading the Bible. The slave preacher could read the Bible. They read the Bible and read something different, and say no – liberation theology – 'We should be free.' They didn't take the standard thing they were told to do; they transformed it.

Slave preachers were also the only people who could travel around the plantations freely, to go to minister. That's why the slave preacher often led the rebellion. Most of the time, 90 per cent of slaves didn't do that; they just did what they were meant to do. But he said (and I paraphrase), 'You're in a position where you have the privileges in order to foment revolution.' And Sam Sharpe's right. This is the only metaphor; this is the way I can justify the professor; this is what Black studies should do, right? Use that position to use those advantages. There is no other job that I could do and get away with whatever things I do. Time-wise, money-wise and resources, this is where I have more access to resources in my position than most people do. And so it's incumbent upon me then to use that to bring down the house. That's the idea of the slave preacher.

Unfortunately, if you do this work too much, you can often become the problem. I went to a university in America with a reputation for being radical. There's me, the head of the department and a young academic from somewhere else, and the head of the department said, 'We forgot that we had a grant of $675,000 from last year.' Forgot! They have so much money they forgot they had a grant. I don't even know what that means! He goes to all the departments and says: 'Have $75,000 spending on what you like (has to be research).' Half of them can't even think of anything to spend it on, right? That's how comfortable they become. The worst part of the story is the young academic. The first thing he says is, 'Oh, that's crazy; I would have bought some furniture for my office.' I had a moment. I left the place depressed. That's why I always say African American studies is not the model that we're looking for. Because of all the resources, all the money, all the things, you could do anything you want. Imagine having that many resources, and that's what you do: you buy furniture for your office. Imagine those resources with the field negro mentality. Imagine what the modern-day Sam Sharpe would do with that. That's what's a positive. We are in these places; we are here – we have prestige and also stress; there is no other job that's better. There is no other job to give you the freedom to do the things that we have. The problem is we don't tend to use it in the way that we should be using it. But Sam Sharpe's a perfect model, so we use that position to subvert the houses of white institutions. That's why I say we're not trying to decolonize the university. We are colonizing the university, drawing out those resources so we can fundamentally bring down the house. That's why I think the spirit of Sam Sharpe is so important.

Notes

1 'The Ballot or the Bullet' can be accessed and listened to through online streaming sites such as YouTube, for example: https://www.you tube.com/watch?v=8zLQLUpNGsc (accessed 26.5.23).

2 'Message to the Grassroots' can be accessed and listened to through online streaming sites such as YouTube, for example: https://www. youtube.com/watch?v=a59Kwp35Z80 (accessed 26.5.23).

3 A painting by Andre Normil (1990) of Haitians performing 'Bwa Kayiman' at the *Ceremonie du Bois-Caiman*, a meeting of slaves considered to be Haiti's first major collective uprising against slavery.

4 Dadzie, Stella (2020), *A Kick in the Belly*, London: Verso Press.

5 'Bun it' is a patois phrase from Jamaica (used colloquially in Black Britain), which in simple terms means 'burn it'.

6 James, C.L.R. (1938/2001), *The Black Jacobins: Toussaint L'Ouverture and the San Domingo Revolution*, London: Penguin Books.

7 Carmichael, S. (Kwame Ture) (2007), *Stokely Speaks: From Black Power to Pan-Africanism*, 1st edn, Chicago, IL: Chicago Review Press.

8 Andrews, Kehinde (2013), *Resisting Racism: Race, Inequality, and the Black Supplementary School Movement*, London: Trentham Books.

9 Available at: https://www.search.birminghamimages.org.uk/details. aspx?ResourceID=4454&ExhibitionID=3503&SearchType=2&Theme ID=403#top (accessed 30.5.23).

10 Andrews, Kehinde (2019), *Back to Black: Retelling Black Radicalism for the 21st Century*, London: Bloomsbury Publishing.

11 Davis, Carole Boyce (2010), *Claudia Jones: Beyond Containment*, Banbury: Ayebia Clarke Publishing.

12 Kiesha Blain's recent texts include *Until I am Free: Fannie Lou Hamer's Enduring Message to America* (2021), Boston, MA: Beacon Press; and *Set the World on Fire: Black Nationalist Women and the Global Struggle for Freedom* (2018), Philadelphia, PA: University of Pennsylvania Press.

13 Stella Dadzie has also written *Toolkit for Tackling Racism in Schools* (2000), Stoke-on-Trent: Trentham Books.

2

Setting the Captives Free: Forging the Paths to Freedom

Amanda Khozi Mukwashi, 2021

The Ideology and Injustice of Racism

I have not come to lecture Black people about the state of our captivity, nor have I come to lecture white people on the state of their privilege. Rather, I have come to call for racial justice as a key first step to social, climate and economic justice and freedom. Racism is an ideology that has been used for centuries to shape the relationships between Black people and people of other skin colours across the world. An ideology that has defined who is human and who is subhuman, whose knowledge is valued and whose is not, and whose lives matter and whose do not. Racism is a belief system that has influenced policies, shaped structures and strengthened the evolution of a capitalist system that has centralized power and wealth in the hands of one social group at the expense of another. This ideology must be dismantled. In the words of Emperor Haile Selassie of Ethiopia, in his address to the United Nations in 1963, 'Until the philosophy which holds one race superior, and another inferior is finally and permanently discredited and abandoned ...'[1] there will be no justice, no freedom and no human rights. These words remind us that a resistance against the union of power and discrimination has been an ancient struggle. For example, the biblical story of Shadrach, Meshach and Abednego (Dan. 3) tells us that, in the midst of flames and fire, these men refused to bow down to idols. Instead, they resisted and remained faithful to their knowledge of who God is. The racial flames today support an ideology that perpetuates a system in which Black bodies have lower status and are ranked at the bottom end of society. This is an ideology that must be permanently discredited and abandoned.

This year's Sam Sharpe Lecture is being hosted in partnership with the Black and Ethnic minority parliamentary caucus. Thank you. This is very welcome. Parliament – the heart and symbol of British democracy – where the voices and freedoms of every British person are guaranteed without fear or favour. However, it is not every British person that enjoys the benefits of these freedoms and not every British voice is heard. Black people have a different experience. Please note that while I speak of the Black experience in this lecture, we must remain aware of the diversities in the Black experience. Black people all experienced subjugation and oppression, and while that is a common thread in their experiences of the relationship with the empire, not all have the history of the transatlantic slave trade.

Nevertheless, the systems, structures, policies and values that started with slavery have progressively been consolidated to keep the poorest and most vulnerable in the chains of poverty and injustice. The majority of these people are Black and Brown people. We are still not free. We must forge the path to freedom and be clear as to what will define our generation as our unique contribution to the liberation of Black people – and it is here that I want to offer some suggestions on how we build on the legacies of those who have gone before us and disrupt the systematic norms until change comes. The racialization of capitalism is a system that must end, but first let us go back together in history and remember the giants who have made it possible for us to be having these conversations in this context.

The Freedom Bearers – the Abolitionists

It is 2021, slavery was abolished in the 1800s, and political independence was gained by former colonies in the 1900s. Sojourner Truth, and those who came after her, struggled for the liberation of Black Africans who were incarcerated in open prisons, otherwise known as plantations. Many whose names must be called, lest we forget their sacrifice, died trying to pave the way to freedom. Names – some of which will never be known or heard of because they simply disappeared and are still missing in action. The tombstones that must be erected in every country, in those countries that participated in the trans-atlantic slave trade and in those countries whose people who were taken and/or sold into slavery must stand tall with no names but the words 'They paved the way to freedom'. We need those tombstones as

- a reminder of the sacrifice that was made for us to be free;
- a warning to generations to come that we have walked this path before and there is only one place it leads to, and that place is not life; and
- a baton for us to run the next stage of the race and to do so with grace and humility.

Many years ago, I worked for the Common Market for Eastern and Southern Africa: a young graduate full of excitement and dreams of a vibrant African continent. I went to Ghana for a meeting that was organized by the Third World Network, where we were discussing trade liberalization and the unfair trade rules that impacted African farmers and other businesses. During my stay in Accra, I had the opportunity to visit Cape Coast Castle. There I found the 'Door of No Return' – a symbol of pain where those captured would 'walk' through to board the ships that would tear them away from everything they knew and take them to a place where their identity would be destroyed for ever, that is, if they survived the journey. What is known is that millions of people were taken, and millions more died on the way. For over 300 years, white Europeans, driven by a belief that Africans were subhuman, created a system that treated humans of a different skin colour as less than wild animals. From Britain, ships left the ports of Liverpool, Bristol and Glasgow to trade in human life, making their owners wealthy and, through the labour of the slaves, contributing to the prosperity of the British public purse – one of the wealthiest public purses in the world today. The battle for freedom from enslavement would be long and hard, and many lives would be lost.

Eventually, the transatlantic slave trade was banned. When the roll is called, let the names of those who struggled for freedom be called: Sojourner Truth and Harriet Tubman searched for freedom. Mary Prince, Ottobah Cugoano, Olaudah Equiano, Phyllis Wheatley, and countless other Black abolitionists, whose names and stories are not mentioned, campaigned for the end of slavery. The immoral nature of the business eventually permeated through to enough people in power and to influencers who then stood together with Black abolitionists and forced the end of the slave trade.

Two key things to note are:

- following the banning of slavery, former slave owners and their descendants were compensated to such an extent that British taxpayers only finished paying this off less than ten years ago;
- most Christian denominations supported the slave trade. Some, like the Quakers and the Church of England, held slaves and financially profited from the trade at some point in their history.

The church was against the abolishing of slavery – just in case we forget and find ourselves being on the wrong side of justice once again in our lifetime. With the abolition of slavery, we had passed through another *door of no return*, even though slavery continued for years after Britain abolished it, including in British colonies. Sadly, slavery continues to this day. The *door of no return* must become a symbol and reminder for us – that never again must we allow our humanity and birthright of freedom to be traded in the public square of capitalism and greed. We owe it to ourselves, to those who have gone and to those who are yet to come. I left Cape Coast Castle in tears and determined that one day I, too, would be counted among those who searched for and stood up for justice and freedom.

But freedom would come in bits. Never freely given. Always fought for. First, they came to take the people away. Then, when trading in human life was no longer acceptable, they came for those left at home; they came for the land and the resources that lay therein. While I am not of the generation that lived under the bonds of colonialism, I was born close enough as part of the post-independence generations who heard the stories first-hand from those who lived through it. Stories of not being allowed in the same church building as white believers and having to stand outside to listen to the word of God. Stories of being treated as subhuman in one's own home. While the shackles had been removed from those who had been transported to the US and the West Indies, those chains had simply been transferred to those who remained on the continent of Africa. *Gold, God and Glory.* The story of colonialism was not just about gold but as aptly and vividly portrayed in Danai Gurira's play *The Convert;*[2] it was a story of religious, cultural and linguistic colonialism too. In just 100 years, the continent would be stripped of what remained of its wealth, spiritual foundations and material possessions; the people subjugated and oppressed – at home. Or at least that is what the colonizing powers attempted to do, and they succeeded to a large extent. But as we have learnt over generations, a lesson we must never forget to pass on to our children is that even in chains our spirit and resilience were not and must never be completely crushed. Traditional warriors, pastoralists, farmers and women fought against the Italians and were successful after five years of struggle. Ethiopia was never colonized, despite the Italians having a narrative that teaches otherwise. As a cradle of civilization, their spirit and resilience won the day. As the apostle Paul says in his second letter to the Corinthians, 'We are hard pressed on every side, but not crushed; perplexed, but not in despair; persecuted, but not abandoned; struck down, but not destroyed' (2 Cor. 4.8–9). New freedom fighters emerged.

The Political Freedom Fighters – the Colonial Activists

Marcus Garvey, Kwame Nkrumah, Kenneth Kaunda and many others learned from and leveraged the gains of the anti-slavery movement and fought for the political freedom of colonized countries. While slavery physically removed people from all they knew and transported them across the oceans, colonialism made Black Africans prisoners in their homeland. The story of the Israelites in the Hebrew Bible bears some interesting parallels to the plight that the people of Africa found themselves in following the abolition of the slave trade. Captives in their own land had no say, no power and no authority over their land, resources or their personhood. Even their knowledge of who they were, and their heritage, was discredited. The wave of independence from colonial rule in Africa brought with it self-rule. The fact that self-rule was based on the colonizers' rules of engagement and that the benchmark of what was good and acceptable was also based on the colonizer as a symbol of what is right, good and ideal is a problem that continues to hold us captive to this day. Key to that is the work of the missionaries and the education systems they set up to convert people to Christianity. The role of the church, once again, in using religion as a tool of oppression that served those with power and wealth, must not be glazed over or rationalized as anything but. Instead, there must be an acknowledgement of wrongs committed, and forgiveness must be sought; restoration is a *sine qua non* for reconciliation. Lessons must be learnt.

Political independence did not come with economic freedom, nor, indeed, with mental freedom. Gold now solidly resided in the coffers of the West, and their museums were now home to cultural and religious artefacts deemed evil by western missionaries but happily providing a source of income and entertainment. Unsure of our footing, our identity was in flux – what did it mean to be a Black African? Were our traditions really evil and primitive? Our traditional practices were relegated to 'customary law' to be administered by local courts, and yet the question must be asked, 'What is English common law if not a set of agreed traditions, practices and behaviours?' We were not free. As Bob Marley, the Jamaican reggae musician, urged us, we needed to free ourselves from mental slavery, even as we walked through yet another *door of no return* – to reclaim our identity, freedom and dignity.

The Post-independence and Neocolonialism Activists

As the world moved from slavery to colonialism and then to modern-day systems – namely neocolonialism – it is important to explore the question of whether these systems were dismantled as new ones came into effect. So, for example, when slavery was abolished, were the structures of power dismantled to allow those who had been oppressed to take their rightful place in the cycle of power and decision-making? Were global financial systems restructured to create a fair and level playing field for international trade and competition? To this end, were new and just financial redistribution systems set up to compensate and restore to those who had been oppressed, whose labour had been exploited and whose bodies dehumanized? In short, were the structures that thrived under the slave systems tackled in order to level up? Or did the colonial system simply build on the previous systems, structures and resources to create a world that looked different and felt different but essentially remained the same? The core engine of the colonial system, the principles and the values that drove that system and ensured that it succeeded were all still very much based on the exploitation of Black people wherever they were – Africa, the Caribbean and the US. So, while colonial administration eventually came to an end, captivity did not. When Africans took over leadership, they took over economies that were set up to serve the needs of former colonial economies. To quote one student from the University of Tennessee:

> European powers pursued this goal by encouraging the development of a commodity-based trading system, a cash crop agriculture system, and by building a trade network linking

the total economic output of a region to the demands of the colonizing state. The development of colonialism and the partition of Africa by the European colonial powers arrested the natural development of the African economic system.[3]

A trend, I am afraid to say, that has come back through Chinese investment in many developing countries. But that is a conversation for another day.

The global trading system, and the regulations around taxation, for example, are decided by the most powerful nations to serve their economies. The legacy of colonialism has therefore taken hold with deep roots in all areas of human life! It ensures that the slave master and the colonizer (one and the same) still have power over Black nations and their wealth-creating systems. They still have a hold over Black knowledge, over what is valued. Still determine how much we are worth. Still refuse to effect reparations for lives and resources lost. Still hold Black lives as inconsequential, Black pain as meaningless and Black personhood as second class. George Floyd.

Maldonado Torres, a South American decolonial theorist, explains this in a different way and uses the concept of coloniality to highlight the impact of colonialism.

Coloniality is different from colonialism. Colonialism denotes a political and economic relations in which the sovereignty of a nation or a people rests on the power of another nation which makes such a nation an empire. Coloniality, instead, refers to long-standing patterns of power that emerged as a result of colonialism (and slavery), but that define culture, labour, inter-subjectivity relations and knowledge production well beyond the strict limits of colonial administrations. Coloniality outlives colonization. It is maintained alive in books, in the criteria of academic performance, culture patterns, in common sense, in the self-image of people, in aspirations of self, and so many other aspects of our modern experience. In a way, as modern subjects, we breathe coloniality all the time and every day.[4]

Slavery, as well as colonialism, are both prequel systems to coloniality.

Those systems have continued to be refined over time so that they have the appearance of being good, fair and not based on race, but the reality is that the economic systems that exist today are still the very same ones that made slavery and colonialism flourish, and until those structures and systems are completely dismantled and changed, Black people will remain in captivity. Captive to economic systems that are hardwired from generations back to keep us in poverty and without equal and fair access to opportunities. Captive to social systems that, in this country, tell us that the benchmark of what is good, what is right and what is desired is white. Social systems that are based on single-source knowledge that has been passed on from generation to generation, social systems, including religions, continue to imply through actions that Black people are an inferior group of people, undeserving of equal consideration as their white counterparts. The history of liberation movements would suggest to us that we must find ways to free ourselves from this captivity and forge pathways to freedom. We need a level playing field. And that means that somewhere else there has to be a giving up of resources, power and blindness/ignorance and space. We must build on the gains of those who have gone before to fight for freedom. But ours is an increasingly difficult task because, just as we must build on the gains that have been made, the current capitalist system is built on the blood of the millions that have died trying to search for freedom and dignity. And yet we must do both: dismantle the system of oppression as we build a system that upholds the dignity of every human being regardless of colour, one that is just and that will ensure generations to come can exist and thrive within planetary boundaries.

The refusal by those who govern to engage in conversations on decolonization, reparations and the institutionalization of racism is disappointing at best and irresponsible and short-sighted at worst. This denial is no different from those who, for the last so many years, have been in denial about the existence of the true nature of climate change – believing instead that humanity can recklessly consume the abundance of the planet without consequence. That those who have benefited the most from climate change, just like those who benefited the most from slavery, colonialism and ongoing capitalism, are somehow exempt from a duty and responsibility to champion the levelling up that is a must-happen in this country and globally and in this generation. To compensate, to pay back, to invest or to restore – I am really not too concerned about the words here. It is the outcome that I am interested in. We need the conversation to move from a battle of definitions to a reality of actions. We need physical freedom, political freedom, economic freedom, social and spiritual freedom. Only then can we say there has been true emancipation and levelling up.

In the last year, some of the superficial varnishes that cover the structures, the mechanisms and the systems of power and wealth have been removed, and we have seen the ugly face of a global system of apartheid. One that has graded human beings according to the colour of their skin and given them a value. The events that have unfolded in the last 18 months leave no one in any doubt as to what value Black and Brown people are given in the bigger scheme of economics. The death of George Floyd in the United States of America, a very public and blatant abuse of privilege, shocked many of us; despite this not being the first time such violence has been meted out to Black people in the US, it was nevertheless very shocking and sent a chill of fear into all of us. While in the US it was death by the hand of a public official that shocked us, in the UK we were waking up to the reality that Black and Brown people were more likely to die of Covid than any other group. That Black and Brown people sat at the bottom of the socio-economic ladder, and the system did not seem to be too concerned. The denial by the report on racism produced by No. 10 that there was no institutional racism in the UK, together with the support for the booing of those taking a knee by the leadership, was an extremely low moment in the history of civilized twenty-first-century Britain.

But I think it is fair to say it has been the management of the vaccine distribution that has removed all doubt. In a recent article, Kevin Watkins, former CEO of Save the Children UK, states:

> Although science and industry have given us the means to immunize the world, nine months after the first arm was jabbed with a Covid-19 vaccine, rich countries are using their market power to direct doses away from poor countries, placing millions of lives at risk. Consider some recent actions by the European Union.

His article goes on to say:

> Under a contract with Johnson & Johnson (J&J), the bloc has imported millions of vaccine doses from a company in South Africa – a country where a mere 11% of the population is vaccinated, and the Delta variant is fueling a surge in cases. Yet efforts to divert vaccine exports from Europe to South Africa and its neighbours were met with a display of vaccine gunboat diplomacy, with the EU threatening to take action under a clause in the J&J contract prohibiting export restrictions.[5]

And while it is difficult for the EU to see Africa and Africans as deserving of consideration, it is easy for the UK to find enough vaccines to trade with Australia and commit millions of vaccines. The economic structures and systems that the western world relies on to maintain power and wealth are supported by the proceeds of the three pillars of slavery: colonialism and capitalism equal coloniality.

It is arguable that capitalism has been the accompanying ideology and common thread that has helped crystallize racism. As part of its own logic of accumulation, capitalism racialized people to map ideas of property and ownership. For slavery and colonialism did more than take life and resources: they destroyed the personhood of the Black individual and collective. They removed the contents and filled the person with information that was meant to 'steal, kill and destroy'. They have held Black people in bondage to this day. Knowledge that came through generations of lived experiences, wisdom that built on ancient knowledge that safeguarded planetary life and identity, were deemed as evil, pagan and primitive, repugnant to natural justice. The yardstick of what was right and good became white and, ever since, we have been chasing our tails, trying to achieve whiteness and everything it stands for. We measure our beauty against whiteness. We measure our success against western benchmarks of success.

Our books sustain this captivity that racism places us in by centring white western voices, stories and experiences – the history of Africa, for example, is only ever told as starting from the arrival of Europeans. The criteria of academic performance sustain this captivity by demanding that children growing up in former British colonies be more proficient in English than their own mother tongue to be able to have better academic and social prospects (another 100 years and the face of language in Africa and everything that is conveyed through it will be lost). Cultural patterns also sustain this captivity through the language we use for who is an 'immigrant' and who is an 'expat'. What do these things tell us about who and what is important? What implications does this have on the path we are to forge towards freedom today?

We plan development and measure progress against western standards. Even when it is becoming increasingly clear that western development is not the answer that is fit for purpose as it is founded on the destruction of both people and planet, still we are hardwired to turn a blind eye to the evident and very real faults of an oppressive system. As people and planet are plundered, Black people around the world are the trampling ground for both. We must create wide spaces to walk through. No more doors. So how do we forge the path ahead?

Forging the Path to Freedom – What Will Define Our Generation?

The question is, what must we do to level the playing field? To break the bonds that keep us out of opportunities, stop us from being in the running and prevent us from having life and having it in its fullness? How do we honour those who have lost their lives for our freedom? Those who didn't make it across the fields? What have we learnt along the way, what type of strategies are required to throw off the twenty-first-century shackles, and what batons are we passing on to the next generation, such as the three lions? These are rhetorical questions we continue to ask ourselves as we reflect on how we continue in the struggle; the answer cannot be provided by one voice alone but in our collective and shared vision of change.

Today we celebrate the Sam Sharpe story as a story of liberation, resilience, activism and faith. While there are many stories of courage and resilience, such as Sam Sharpe, Harriet Tubman and others, our trauma remains as we remember that over 1.5 million Black bodies suffered during the middle passage and remain missing in action, but how many Black bodies are missing in action today and how do we, like Sam Sharpe, keep forging ahead and building new pathways for the generations to come? Most African and Caribbean populations living in the diaspora have (for the most part) developed a level of resilience so as to survive; for example, think of the Black footballers in the England squad.

Every generation has left a legacy behind. For those who fought slavery, they focused on physical freedom. Those who challenged colonialism were looking for political independence. For our generation, we too must ask ourselves what our legacy will be. Just like those who have travelled this road before us, we need to pick our game changer – the battleground for our investments, our thinking and our knowledge. There are many things that we can all do to improve things: policies, legislation, economics, education, rights and more. What will be our 'slavery was abolished' or 'we gained political independence' moment? What will define our generation as our unique contribution to the liberation of Black people – forging the path to freedom? Can we build a new house on the same foundation as the old one while trying to dismantle it?

There are two cathedrals in Coventry that stand side by side. One is a ruin that remained from the Second World War when it was bombed. Coventry was flattened, and this cathedral was almost completely crushed. Bits of the walls of the cathedral remained standing, and the cross that stood where the altar must have been still stands to this day. Next to this burnt-down cathedral, a new one has been built. A modern building that now attracts visitors from all around the world. A symbol of peace and reconciliation. Perhaps we, too, must build a new society that is founded on the human rights declaration, where all people enjoy the same rights and freedoms and where every human being is created in the image of God and deserving of dignity. It can be done. But to do this we must create opportunities for ourselves in this generation and for generations to come. Our battleground is opportunity – opportunity to free ourselves from economic and social bondage, opportunity that celebrates Black talents, values that are on a par with white talent in all disciplines and innovation, and then reward it in equal measure. And so, allow me to make some suggestions where I see opportunities.

Securing Space, Voice and Opportunities for Future Generations

The opportunity for everyone to do their duty and responsibility. Every leader, every parent, and every citizen to ensure that we create a space where freedom and justice reign

'Change comes through continuous struggle' (Dr Martin Luther King Jr) and 'Keep Hope Alive' are slogans and chants of the 1960s Civil Rights Movement, chanted to remind the membership to march forward in the face of discrimination and unjust legal systems. We, too, struggle for what is just. That is how we honour the lives that have gone before us and how we pave the way for those coming behind. We march and stand together. The Black Lives Matter protests that took place across the world last year were different in that they were not only about Blackness: the protests were about justice. Images of young people from all walks of life, different skin colours holding banners and marching side by side defied the notion that this is a Black-people fight only. Black Lives Matter was a clear message: we cannot sit and watch while some houses on the street burn to ashes because of a system that we have created. In the same way, we cannot sit and do nothing while climate change, caused by our actions, impacts the most vulnerable in many countries and threatens their very existence. We must do this together. We must deliberately walk away from the individualism of opportunities and instead collectivize our struggles for justice, dignity and equality. This time around, we must either walk through the door of no return together or create wider spaces for us all to walk through.

We need, therefore, to be better represented in public life and public policy mechanism. For example, since the publication of the Stephen Lawrence Inquiry Report, there have been numerous initiatives, policies and guidance documents published, aimed at improving performance across and within the criminal justice system. Some progress has been made, but there is still much more that needs to happen to eliminate institutional racism.

The opportunity to restore that which has been buried: knowledge

In my book *But Where Are You Really From?*,[6] I belabour the point on identity and the different elements that make me who I am. They are all equally important and contribute to my personhood. We must not be afraid to place in our education systems and, for those like me who work in the development and humanitarian sector, to inform our understanding with the information and knowledge that comes from different sources, told in different ways and placing different interpretations in the cradle of learning. As we acquire new knowledge, we must be mindful that this new knowledge is subject to the same burying processes that prioritize certain types of knowledge from particular places and geographies. Therefore, locating the practices and systems that bury the knowledge is key to changing it and forging a pathway to true knowledge. Only then can we claim to be knowledgeable and educated. For now, those who claim to be the echelons of education systems are simply the repositories of one world view – a very limited understanding of the world indeed. The ranking of educational institutions should be based on more than this. Rather, we must look to those whose insecurities do not stand in the way of true learning. The notion that before Europeans came to Africa, Black people were uncivilized would be laughable, but for the untold damage it has done to the earth's inhabitants. Knowledge has been buried and must be restored for all to learn from, unlearn and relearn. *All.* Then we can begin to create the wide spaces to walk on.

The opportunity to forgive, repent, restore and reconcile

For any people who have been at the receiving end of wrong-doing, the path to peace requires forgiveness, repentance and restoration and leads to reconciliation. The continual denial of successive British governments to engage with the dark past of the British Empire, the refusal to acknowledge the merci-less plundering and looting of resources and causing of loss of millions of lives, is to perpetuate the abhorrent notion of Black people as subhuman. We can learn from what has been done before. In September 1951, Chancellor Konrad Adenauer of West Germany addressed his parliament:

> unspeakable crimes have been committed in the name of the German people, calling for moral and material indemnity ... The Federal Government are prepared, jointly with represent-atives of Jewry and the State of Israel ... to bring about a solu-tion of the material indemnity problem, thus easing the way to the spiritual settlement of infinite suffering.[7]

Abhorrent crimes against humanity were committed against Black people in Africa, the US, the UK and the Caribbean, the suffering of which continues to this day. Matthew, a disciple of Jesus Christ, writes of a story that Jesus told of the servant who had been taken from his master. The servant not only apologized but committed to restore that which had been taken. Perhaps that example does not sit well with those who might question that the British Empire was not a servant. Well, then, the tax collector asks Jesus what he must do regarding all those whom he has robbed. And Jesus responds and asks him to restore fourfold. Financial restitution must be made to the nations whose people were traded and whose resources were plundered and destroyed. This will not heal the broken spirit of nations, but it will be a key step in forging the path to freedom and dignity for all, not only Black people but all people. We need to create the opportunity to forgive, to repent, to restore and to reconcile. All of creation needs it. Our continued failure to see this is destroying our planet and everything and everyone in it.

The opportunity to 'Proclaim freedom for the captives' (Isa. 61.1 and Luke 4.18)

Christians speak about the work of Christ, but a gap remains in living out the teaching and actions of Christ. Too often churches have been silent and complicit. Christianity has been shaped by the assumptions of a religion that has been propped up by empire. What is required of us is a need to call out and reject the gospel of Caesar parading as the gospel of Jesus. We are called to be prophetic and proactive on issues of justice and reconciliation. For Black Christians, I say this to you; Scripture records that those who were born in bondage in Egypt did not get to the promised land, but generations after did. It was those in bondage who took the first step. Each generation must take its first step. If faith matters, then Christianity has to make sense to me as a Black African, in my context and in my space and in my language. We need, therefore, to free ourselves from what Christian Aid has called an 'unquenchable thirst', a spirit of greed and a character of instant gratification with no thought for the future. Seek the peace of the land and reject a framing that focuses on accessing unlimited resources, which in turn is connected to global capitalism and a discourse that supports the exploitation of people, land and services.

Conclusion

Let me leave you with this message. One thing that climate change and the Covid pandemic have both shown the world today – if we are paying attention – is that we are in captivity as humanity. We are in an escape room, and each group/section of society holds different clues that need to be used together if we are to get out alive – all of us. The continued meting out of injustice on the most vulnerable, on Black people and on those most marginalized is not sustainable and will ultimately lead to the destruction of the world as we know it.

As we close, allow me to give thanks for Sam Sharpe, who passed on the baton of freedom to our generation. 'Let us not become weary in doing good, for at the proper time we will reap a harvest if we do not give up' (Gal. 6.9). Allow me also to urge us all not to let the struggles and the gains of those who have gone before us be for nought. But with love, faith and hope, let us persevere in our pursuit of freedom. The prophet Isaiah says in chapter 61.1:

> The Spirit of the Lord GOD is upon me, because the LORD hath anointed me to preach good tidings unto the meek; he hath sent me to bind up the brokenhearted, to proclaim liberty to the captives, and the opening of the prison to them that are bound.

Be free. Thank you.

Notes

1 Spoken to the United Nations General Assembly on 4 October 1963, and often considered inspiration for Bob Marley and the Wailers' song 'War', 1976.

2 Gurira, Danai (2017), *The Convert*, London: Oberon Books.

3 Settles, Joshua Dwayne (1996), 'The Impact of Colonialism on African Economic Development', Chancellor's Honors Program Projects. Available at: https://trace.tennessee.edu/utk_chanhonoproj/182 (accessed 2.6.23).

4 'On the Coloniality of Being', *Cultural Studies* 21.2, pp. 240–70. To link to this article: DOI: 10.1080/09502380601162548, p. 243.

5 See www.project-syndicate.org/commentary/ending-trickle-down-vaccine-economics-by-kevin-watkins-2021-09 (accessed 2.6.23).

6 Mukwashi, Amanda Khozi (2020), *But Where Are You Really From?*, London: SPCK.

7 *Treaties and International Agreements Filed and Recorded from 20 March 1953 to 31 March 1953*, United Nations Treaty Series (in English and French), vol. 162, pp. 205–311.

3

Man Against the System

Bishop Wilton Powell, 2020

The emerging world view emanating from the Renaissance and Reformation established a world order that came to be known as western civilization. This world order was underpinned by a social, political and economic foundation of capitalism. Historically, western civilization as an expression of European thoughts has shaped political, economic, technological development, religious, philosophical and moral considerations worldwide. Samuel P. Huntington argues that both civilization and culture refer to the overall way of life and people.[1]

Although western civilization took ideological perspectives and intentions from previous civilizations – Chinese, Greek, Roman and others – there is no doubt that the ascendency of the West has profoundly influenced human lives in the last 500 years. It is the intention of this lecture to examine how western civilization impacted the lives of African people in the enterprise known as the transatlantic slave trade. Before proceeding any further, I do believe that it is important that a political context be established. It is Jean-Jacques Rousseau who said that 'man was born free but is everywhere in chains'.[2] Rousseau's agreements were directed against the privileges of kingship and the nobilities of Europe. As the Renaissance flourished, it can be seen that Rousseau, Thomas Hobbs and others had parallel thoughts as they strived to assert the inalienable rights of man.[3] Their political thoughts set the context for a social contract that would preserve the common good. It was from this political perspective that the culmination of these political writings reflected the Utopian ideas of the Enlightenment. In Thomas

Paine's book *The Rights of Man*, common sense clearly exerts the privileges of man. Paine believed that the mind, once enlightened, cannot again become darkened. There is no possibility, nor are there any terms to express, this supposition of the mind unknowing anything it already knows. In keeping with this new optimism, his *Rights of Man* and other works present America as setting the example the rest of the world will follow.[4]

The European believed that to be enlightened was the state of being that reflected the modern state of development (of philosophy, technology, politics, economics and all the other components that sustain the infrastructure of the new European culture). But this new culture was founded upon secular humanism, and this perspective gave the church meaning to the temporal realm or the world political realm as opposed to the spiritual realm and church tradition.[5] Many perceive western civilization to be primarily influenced by Christianity, yet there were scientific principles offered by Darwinism that suggest alternative pathways of human development other than the Judaeo-Christian world view where all men are made in the image of God.[6] Jacob Bronowski, who speaks about the 'ascent of man', captures the essence of the ascendancy of European civilization. He says that revelations are not made by fate but by men, and what drove them was the conviction that man is the master of his own salvation.[7]

As we shall see, the classical writers speak of man or mankind, but in the colonial enterprise mankind was classified as white Europeans and others, who were not enlightened, civilized or uncivilized. Throughout human history, people have always been enslaved, but it is only in western civilization that people were enslaved because of race and colour.[8] Huntington has highlighted that in the early nineteenth century, the concept of race played an increasing role in scientific, intellectual and popular thinking in both Europe and America. The extent to which this belief and practice are seen within European civilization is clearly manifested in Dred Scott's court case in 1857. Chief Justice Rodger B. Taney's opinion for Dred Scott's case held that the constitution assumed that not just slaves but all Blacks were a subordinated and inferior class of beings, unentitled to the rights and liberties of citizens and hence not part of the people of the United States. This decision was abrogated by the fourteenth amendment in 1968, which declared that all persons born or neutralized in the United States were citizens of the United States.[9] The entire slave-owning and colonization enterprise was primarily directed towards property acquisitions, although the constitution of the United States proclaimed the equality of all men in their rights and freedom.

In *Civilization: The West and the Rest*, Niall Ferguson argues that in the US constitution, for all its many virtues and institutionalized strength, the division of races and accepting the legitimacy of slavery was the original sin of the new republic.[10] This amendment to the constitution created a facility that enabled Black people to be treated as property or commodities. The evidence supporting the above position by a South Carolina representative in Congress was determined according to rules that a slave or other persons in the constitution's language should be counted as three-fifths of a man.[11] Ferguson, having observed the inconsistencies between the classic political and philosophical thoughts, the framers of the American constitution, and political pragmatism in creating *dislocation* between human people groups (separating whites from the Black race), concluded that there is a paradox at the heart of western civilization.[12] I believe it was this paradox to which Professor J. M. Roberts was referring when he said that there was a flaw in western civilization.[13]

It is clear that western civilization created boundaries in the human species that separated the enlightened European from other men, particularly those of African descent. If we accept the concept that western civilization is a definition of modernity, an ascendant cultural way of living, then there is a support proposition that this state existed only for Europeans. Fischer argues that the real problem, it seems to him, is with *accounts* of modernity as an a posteriori theorization of perhaps even part of a strategy that aims to establish European primacy.[14]

Slave Society (Sam Sharpe's World)

The characteristics of slave society stand in a very steep contrast to the world of European civilization and culture, where political thinkers seek to establish the inalienable rights of man. In the slave society, he was considered less than human and did not have the privilege of human rights. This paradoxical configuration created the resistive stimulus for Sam Sharpe's rebellion against the plantocracy; therefore, it must be understood that, in this lecture, I would prefer to use Sam Sharpe's name as a metaphor for the resistance of the people against the plantocracy (system). In this instance, plantocracy represents the social, political and economic system that has stolen and transported African people from Africa to the Caribbean and the Americas. I further highlight that the struggle for abolition and emancipation from slavery was a joint venture in that both males and females were agents. Furthermore, the contribution of William Wilberforce and other prominent citizens, who held the Judaeo-Christian world view that all men were created by God equally, added a powerful dynamic to this rebellion.

In *Burning for Freedom*, Delroy Reid-Salmon argues that it is impossible to ignore women as integral entities in the struggle against slavery. Bush provides a descriptive account of slave resistance in two dimensions – individual and collective. She also argues that 'The unifying thread of the individual and the collective dimension of resistance is the African cultural heritage of the slave woman which fired her rebellious spirit, frequently bringing her into conflict with the laws and values of the master-class.'[15] Reid-Salmon says there is a mystery surrounding Sam Sharpe's life, and although there is a scarcity of information on Sharpe's biographical details, it is reasonable to argue that he was intelligent and influential. Reid-Salmon supports this point of view by saying it is arguable that the ability to inspire and persuade others to pursue action they would not have done under normal circumstances attests to the nature of Sharpe's intellect. It may be that the best portrait of Samuel Sharpe's character that we now have is the fictionalized narrative of Fred Kennedy. Sharpe said, 'It seems strange that a slave would write stories, but thanks to the kindness of my master, Samuel Sharpe Esquire, I now possess the ability to read and write and have acquired many other graces of an English gentleman.'[16] However, the slave society to which Sam Sharpe was born was the very antithesis of the enlightened society, the sense of human dignity crushed by the reality of his brutal existence. Sherlock and Bennett argue that 'the society created by sugar was rigid, base and greedy. It consumed life, energy and thought, and manured the industrial revolution of England with profits from its labour.'[17] The economic argument of the profitability and quality of Negro slave labour was woven into the fabric of the plantation strategy, choices and decisions. As Williams argues, 'the colonies needed labour and resorted to Negro labour because it was the cheapest and best. This was not a theory, it was a practical conclusion deduced from the personal experience of the planters'.[18]

There were also factors of management in addition to the economic argument mentioned above; Williams states that racial differences made it easier to justify and rationalize Negro slavery, to exact the mechanical obedience of a plough-ox or carthorse, to demand that resignation and that complete and intellectual subjection which alone make slave labour possible. He further argues that finally, and this was the decisive factor, the Negro slave was cheaper; the money that procured a white man's services for ten years could buy a Negro for life.[19]

Economic efficiency and effectiveness depend upon good government of an economic system. Dr Hilary Beckles argues that the definitive expression of the slave society was first established in Barbados. He further points out that the slave code of 1661 was a defining element within the meaning of the slave society. It was the foundation upon which the social order was articulated and clearly understood. Furthermore, it was the philosophical core of all social and economic relations and defined the totality of political and cultural life. The essence of this slave code, which defines the precise nature, structures and functions of the African man, stands in contrast to the enlightened political and social order that Europe advocated for itself. Whereas slavery had existed before this document, the 1661 code, Beckles's suggestion defines 'the transition from a society that included a minority of enslaved Africans to one conceptualized and built entirely around the legally assured principle of property rights in African bodies was innovative and transformative'.[20]

Slavery and Capitalism: the Transatlantic Slave Trade was an Economic Engine for Capitalism and the Industrial Revolution

Catherine Hall, Nicholas Draper and others, who have written on the subject of colonial slavery and the formation of Victorian Britain, have stated that slave ownership is virtually invisible in British history.[21] The issue of the slave trade in western civilization, particularly in Britain, where the first industrial revolution was initiated, is still a historical embarrassment. Eric Williams argues that the Spanish conquistadors 'brought to the New World an economic and social heritage in which slavery and serfdom were constituent elements'.[22]

For Ferguson, in consideration of the European colonization process, the attitude to conquest was the same. If the initial conditions were determining, then it did not much matter if Englishmen or Spaniards turned up in Peru; the result would have been much the same because the English would have been just as tempted to plunder the Incas and just as likely to succumb to 'resource curse' of cheap gold and silver.[23] Ferguson advocates that there was a systemic aspect to the European approach to colonization. He says:

> the crux of the matter is the relative importance in the historical process of, on the one hand, initial resource endowments in the colonized territories of the New World and, on the other hand, the institutional blueprints the colonizers brought with them from Europe.[24]

The institutional blueprints suggest a form of architectural framework that was sustainable. In the first instance, it was the superiority of their race and culture. This racial superiority became the foundational ideological bedrock of capitalist architecture. Sherlock and Bennett say that most English scholars steadfastly held to these fundamental tenets. Teutonic, and especially Anglo-Saxon, races were superior in all respects, and inferiority could only be ameliorated by tutelage to the former. The French, Dutch, Belgium, Italian and Germans all shared this racial vision.[25] This belief system of intrinsic superiority in European culture permeated all structures, institutions and functions, governments and society in the colonial world. From the perspective of the colonized, they saw commerce, Christianity, civilization and conquest as the factors establishing the new world economic order.[26]

In his preparation to publish his seminal work *Capitalism and Slavery*, Eric Williams believed that slavery in the Caribbean had been too narrowly identified with the Negro. 'A racial twist has thereby been given to what is basically an economic phenomenon.'[27] This business enterprise was developed in accordance with the economic policies of the Stuart monarchy; the slave trade was intrinsic to a monopolistic company, the company of Royal Adventurers trading to Africa, incorporated in 1663 for a period of 1,000 years.

> The monopoly meant the purchase of British manufactures for sale on the coast of Arica, control of ships employed in the slave trade, sale of Negroes to the plantations, importation of the plantation produce – 'this great circle of trade and navigation,' on which the livelihood, direct and indirect, of many thousands depended – would be under the control of a single company.[28]

Capitalism, the Financial Engine of the Industrial Revolution

The national revenue generated by the transatlantic slave trade permeated the entire economic fabric of British society. Williams argues that the triangular trade thereby gave a triple stimulus to British industry. The Negroes were purchased, manufactured and transported to the plantations: 'They produced sugar, cotton, indigo, molasses and other tropical products, the processing of which created new industries in England, while the maintenance of the Negroes and their owners on the plantations provided another market for British industry, New England agriculture and the Newfoundland fisheries.' He further declared, 'By 1750 there was hardly a trading or manufacturing town in England which was not connected with the triangular or direct colonial trade. The profits obtained provided one of the main streams of capital accumulation in England which financed the Industrial Revolution.'[29]

The rise of the wealth and prosperity of the nation made the West Indian islands the financial jewel in their crown. Williams further argues that

> The West Indian islands became the hub of the British Empire, of immense importance to the grandeur and prosperity of England. It was the Negro slaves who made these sugar colonies the most precious colonies ever recorded in the whole annals of imperialism. To Postlethwayt, they were the fundamental prop and support of the colonies, 'valuable people' whose labour supplied Britain with all plantation produce. The British Empire was 'a magnificent superstructure of American commerce and naval power on an African foundation.'[30]

Speaking from the magnificence of the superstructure of the imperial economy, all commentators agreed on the worth of West Indian colonies – Sir Dalby Thomas, Adam Smith, and Sir Charles Whitworth and others.[31]

The Primacy of Freedom: the Abolition of the Caribbean Slave System

The establishment and development of the Caribbean slave system was basically the result, as we have already indicated, of the importance of that system to the economy of the metropolitan government. Conversely, the abolition of the slave system was basically the result of the fact that the system had lost its former importance.[32] Williams gave a perspective of how the slave system of the Caribbean was abolished. He said the slave system was abolished at different times during the nineteenth century throughout the Caribbean. The slave trade was finally abolished by Denmark in 1803, was abolished by Great Britain in 1807 and, though restored by Bonaparte in 1802, was abolished by the French government in 1817.[33]

There were treaties of abolishment established by Great Britain and other countries that had a vested interest in the Caribbean slave system. We can consider the abolition of the Caribbean slave system under the following categories:

- Economic factors.
- Political factors.
- Forces of reformation and justice.
- Humanitarian agitation.
- Social factors.
- International and intercolonial rivalry.

Economic Factors Impacting the Caribbean Slave System

The trends of production in all colonial territories were declining, except for Cuba, on the eve of emancipation. Their economy was bankrupt. There were only three topics of conversation on the islands: debt, disease and death. Between 1799 and 1808, 65 plantations had been abandoned, 32 were sold under orders of the court of chancery to meet claims there, and, in 1807, suits were pending against 115 others.[34]

In 1806, the price of sugar was then the cost of production, and in 1807 the planters made no profit at all. From a metropolitan standpoint, the day's mercantilism was over. The West Indies represented shrinking markets, and they produced more expensive sugar, which competed with that of the better customers of the metropolis. In the case of the British West

Indies, the competitors were India and Brazil.[35] Britain had accumulated great wealth and economic influence globally. The increase of consumption goods called forth by that trade inevitably drew in its train the development of the productive power of the country. This industrial expansion required finance. Williams argues that the eighteenth century was better able to afford the ready capital than a West Indian sugar planter of a Liverpool slave trader.[36]

> We have already noticed the readiness with which absentee planters purchased land in England, where they were able to use their wealth to finance the great developments associated with the Agricultural Revolution. We must now trace the investments of profits from the triangular trade in British industry, where they supplied part of the huge outlay for the construction of the vast plants to meet the needs of the new productive process and the new markets.[37]

Merchant bankers became the great custodians of the wealthier British and commercial strategists for the development of the nation. Typical of the eighteenth-century banker is the transformation from tradesman to merchant, and then the further progression from merchant to banker. In the eighteenth-century context, the term 'merchant' not infrequently involved the gradations of slaver captain, privateer captain and privateer owner, before settling down on the shore to the respectable business of commerce. The varied activities of a Liverpool businessman include brewer, liquor merchant, grocer, spirit dealer, bill-broker and banker, for example. Prominent in Liverpool merchant banking communities were the Heywood Bank and Thomas Parke of the banking firm of William Gregson Sons. 'The emergence of Thomas Leyland on the banking scene was delayed until the early years of the nineteenth century, but his investments in the African slave trade dated back to the last quarter of the eighteenth century.'[38] The knowledge of the decline in the Caribbean slave system must be strategically redirected according to the abiding interest and economic security of the nation.

For London, only one name is mentioned, and that name is Barclay. Two members of this Quaker family, David and Alexander, were engaged in the slave trade in 1756. David began his career in American and West Indian Commerce and became one of the most influential merchants of his day. The rise of banking in Glasgow was intimately connected with triangular trade. The first regular bank began business in 1760, known as the Ship Bank; one of the original partners was Andrew Buchanan, a tobacco Lord of the city.[39]

In the eighteenth century, when the slave trade was the most valuable trade and West Indian property in the British Empire, the triangular occupied an important position in the eyes of the rising insurance companies. In the early years, when Lloyd's was a coffee house and nothing more, many advertisements in the *London Gazette* about runaway slaves listed Lloyd's as the place where they should be returned.[40]

It was clearly recognized that the financial profits from the West Indies were the principal economic thrust that developed the British economy. Abbe Raynal said, the 'West Indies may be considered the principal cause of the rapid motion which now agitates the universe'.[41]

The evidence of this financial benefit in the slave industry in Wales, which provided roofing material, was revolutionized by the new methods adopted on the Caernarvonshire estate by Lord Penrhyn, who owned sugar plantations. These financial supports also went into the large infrastructure projects that made Britain a modern political economy. With the great railway projects, Williams argues in 1783, the shape of things to come was clearly visible. The steam engine *potentialities* were not a question. The results of changes were seen: 66 engines were in operation, and two-thirds of these were in mines and foundries.

Williams argues that the beneficent breath of increased production stimulated the entire economy of England. The output of the Staffordshire potteries increased fivefold in value between 1725 and 1777.[42]

Political Factors Impacting the Caribbean Slave System

The second set of factors in the abolition of the slave system, which we are now to consider, is political. This can be treated under two headings – the metropolitan and the colonial. It was Jean-Jacques Rousseau who argued that 'man was born and is everywhere in chains'.[43] This experience was the reality of the enslaved on the sugar plantations of the Caribbean. In their history of the Jamaican people, Sherlock and Bennett raise the issue of 'the primacy of freedom'.[44] Sherlock and Bennett state that, after Jamaica was captured from the Spaniards in 1656, Major General Robert Sedgwick said, 'the Spaniard is not considerable, but of the Blacks, there are many, who are like to prove as thorns, and pricks in our side'. Some months later, he wrote that 'in two days, more than forty of our soldiers were cut off by the Negros'.[45]

Sherlock and Bennett believe that the Africans of Spanish Jamaica had established the resistance pattern of fugitive slaves based on Palenque, their strongholds of freedom. The English conquest of Jamaica did not mean the conquest of these free Africans nor the destruction of their Palenque.[46] Williams supports the argument of Sherlock and Bennett in highlighting that the English conquest of Jamaica had been followed by the flight of most of the Negroes to the island's interior, where they continued the struggle against the English troops. The pacification of the island was virtually completed in 1657, when the leader of the main body of the Maroons, Juan de Bolas, surrendered to the English in terms of paradox and freedom.[47] Although there were stages in the pacification process by small groups of Negroes who contrived the resistance of the Maroons, there was no alternative but to make peace with the Maroons. The treaty was signed on 1 March 1739. The British had to make terms with a band of rebel slaves whom they had been unable to defeat and subdue. The terms represented the erection of a Maroon state within the colony of Jamaica.[48]

The deep sense of resistance to the plantocracy has never been disputed in the mind of slavery within Jamaica or within the slave system of the Caribbean. Sherlock and Bennett argue that earlier liberation wars had centred on Maroons or plantations in specific parishes. Now freedom for all African-Jamaica-born Blacks was in the majority. All spoke a Jamaican dialect, shared the same creole culture, the same desire for freedom and communicated fully with each other through their folk language. The cultural resonances were engaging with the historical dynamics of political and social resistance. Sherlock and Bennett support the ideology that motivation and assertiveness were found within the slaves in songs. They say work songs recorded in this period reflect a change of mode and a more open mockery of *backra*[49], a growing distrust of him, more frequent references to freedom, and an increasing restiveness.[50] The revolutionary songs were Christian hymns, some of which were introduced by the Black Baptist missionaries and other white Baptist missionaries from Great Britain.[51]

Two strands of the Baptist movement were the primary catalyst for transformation among the enslaved in Jamaica. First, there was the missionary pioneer in western Jamaica, Moses Baker, born in New York and a barber by trade. When the English evacuated New York in 1783, he left with his family as refugees to Kingston. Second, there were missionaries from the Baptist Missionary Society, who responded to an appeal from Baker in 1813 and 1814. Sherlock and Bennett believe that when other English missionaries were beginning to arrive, slave discontent broke into rebellion.[52]

Fundamental to this restive nature among slaves was the theology that promoted the belief that all men were created equal by God and should be treated the same. Revolutionary songs by the enslaved underpinned their egalitarian theological perspective.

Leadership for this rebellion emerged from the Baptist congregations. The degree of resistance in the slave economy was strong and infectious throughout the Caribbean. Williams highlights that there were 13 instances of rebellion between 1733 and 1776. He further adds that Jamaica featured seven times in these rebellions.[53] This restive nature within the Caribbean slave system created an ineffective and inefficient production of sugar.

Sherlock and Bennett highlight a framework of rebellion and emancipation. They conclude that the western liberation uprising of 1832 benchmarks the climax of the African-Jamaicans' struggle against slavery, and the British Parliament's Act of emancipation of 1833. This long conflict was an African response, affirming the right of man to freedom in which the African prevailed. In this fixed phase, although the western liberation uprising failed in its immediate objective, it succeeded in achieving its primary goal of emancipation.[54] They considered Sam Sharpe's rebellion ironic when the question was posed: 'Who would have imagined that the rebel leaders swinging from the gallows in Montego Bay during that agonizing May of 1832 were to become the honoured dead of a predominately African-Jamaican people or that their leader, Sam Sharpe, would be referred to as one of the heroes and creators of the nation?'[55]

Sherlock and Bennett believe that the rebellion led by Sam Sharpe was different from others in respect that they were asking slaves everywhere not to call to arms but to call for a withdrawal of their labour, and it was issued to people who were determined to win their freedom.[56] They also believed that the social dynamics in western Jamaica had moved towards change; Kamau Braithwaite emphasizes that western Jamaica was, by the early years of the nineteenth century, psycho-culturally prepared for revolution against the plantation system.[57] From the 1820s, Sam Sharpe had been talking about locking down all plantations.[58]

Sherlock and Bennett also highlight the logistics and strategy by which such a task could be accomplished. They outline that there was also man and woman power. In the western part of the island (St James, Trelawney, St Elizabeth, Hanover, Westmoreland), where some 30 per cent of all the colony's slaves were concentrated, that is 106,000 out of more than 310,000. Of this, 106,000, between 18,000 and 40,000, were involved in the revolt; among them were urban Blacks and coloured and free Black women, two of whom were executed for their part in the rebellion.[59]

The leaders formed the elite of the labour force, men who had exercised as much authority as a slave could, some of them deacons of the Baptist Church, literate and aware of events in Britain, and especially of the work of the abolitionists. Sam Sharpe planned and led the rebellion.[60]

Forces of Reformation and Justice Impacting the Caribbean Slave System

The Caribbean slave system financed the Industrial Revolution and introduced a new paradigm in European society, the industrial proletariat. Therefore Williams advances the argument that, from the perspective of metropolitan politics, the abolition of the Caribbean slave system was, on the one hand, a part of the struggle of the industrial bourgeoisie against the landed aristocracy, which began in France with the French Revolution of 1789, advanced in England with the first reform bill of 1832, triumphed with the annulment of the English corn laws in 1846, and culminated in the victory of the North over the South in the Civil War in the United States.[61]

The struggle for freedom of the slaves in the Caribbean slave system became one with the United States Civil War for the release of slaves. In recognition of the worldwide paradigm shift for freedom, Williams argues that 'the emancipation of the slaves was a part of the general movement of the European industrial proletariat towards democracy. The centres of the agitation against slavery were the great industrial towns of Britain and France, with Manchester, Birmingham, Sheffield and Paris in the lead.'[62] William Cobbett highlighted the linkage between the working class of Britain and the Caribbean slave system; the working-class leader said that the fruit of slave labour had long been used to make slaves of the British people.[63] However, it is most interesting to see that the reformers, who stood for and activated changes in the Caribbean slave system, were engaged in the advocacy of change in British industrial reform. A small group of activists, known as the Clapham Sect evangelicals, believed in a true expression of their faith for spiritual transformation and social change. Ernest Marshall Howse states that the most permanent element in the Clapham Sect is to be found in the Thornton family. An uncle of William Wilberforce, John Thornton was already living in a spacious mansion in Clapham when, in 1756, Henry Venn, one of the most distinguished of the early evangelicals, began his ministry there.[64]

Humanitarian Agitation Impacting the Caribbean Slave System

There are close relationships to humanitarian agitation and political considerations already mentioned in the activities of the Clapham Sect. Williams highlights that the humanitarian agitation for the abolition of the slave system is associated particularly with the names of Clarkson, Wilberforce and Fowell Buxton in England, and Victor Schoelcher in France.[65]

This section intends to look at the parliamentary activities of those persons mentioned above and their associated colleagues. Planters of the Caribbean slave system had lost their influential position in the public space because of the multiple factors that were now impacting the slave system: the slave rebellions, the overproduction of sugar in the France, Cuba and Brazil regions; the restrictive monopoly of navigational law; diversions of the Industrial Revolution and public repugnance of the slave trade. Williams argues that in the election for the parliament that passed the first reform bill, slavery in the West Indies was a vital issue. 'I am an advocate for the abolition of West Indies slavery,' said Brougham in his campaign in Sheffield, and 'both root and branch, I will tear it up'.[66] The British parliament was at pains to emphasize this interpretation. In the House of Lords, objections were raised to the declaration that the slave trade was contrary to justice and humanity on the grounds that this was a reflection of the slave trader.

The psycho-cultural shift within British society created opportunity. Wilberforce and his colleagues developed strategies for navigating their plans in the Houses of Parliament. Williams argues that, up to this time, the British abolitionists had never supported emancipation. He argues that the circumstances were now much more favourable. Wilberforce rejoiced at the introduction, 'as it gave him an opportunity to oppose it and show the distinction his party had always made between abolition and emancipation. The abolitionists turned their attention to measures calculated to prevent evasion of the abolition act and secure its enforcement.'[67]

Martin Luther King II spoke of speaking to the conscience of the nation – the United States – but in terms of the abolition and emancipation of slavery in the Caribbean slave system and of Sam Sharpe (the slave), and Wilberforce, Granville Sharp and Clarkson, who exerted slave labour as moral leverage. Subsequent legislation making the slave trade a felony and requiring a general registry of the slaves of each colony made evasion of the abolition not difficult.[68]

The internal shortage of slave labour created problems in maintaining the Caribbean slave system. In the face of these problems, Williams argues, specious arguments were used by governors and planters alike to justify and encourage this trade. The most popular was that as Crown colonies without discretion, with respect to the ameliorating measures commanded by the metropolitan government, the slave should be encouraged to migrate to the governing colonies. In this scenario, again, we see how capitalism manipulates the slave system in the interest of the planters and the metropolitan powers. In addition, Williams argues that the superior value of slaves and greater fertility of the soil of Trinidad and Guiana would form the background to this intercolonial slave trade.[69]

Wilberforce and others campaigned for the worldwide abolition of the worldwide trade in slavery. Williams says,

> the campaign against the foreign slave trade failed because British capitalism was heavily interested in trade with Latin America, particularly Brazil and Cuba. It could not kill the goose that laid the golden eggs – that is, it could not oppose the introduction of the slaves who produced the sugar and coffee that made possible the purchase of British textiles and produced freights for British ships.[70]

Social Factors Impacting the Caribbean Slave System

The abolition of the slave trade across the Caribbean created an environment of optimism across the Caribbean, which made it difficult to manage the expectations of the slaves. As stated earlier, Sam Sharpe planned for field slaves to withhold their labour. There was a clear psycho-cultural insight into the minds of the colonial authorities; Governor Combermere of Barbados wrote to the secretary for the colonies in 1819 that, in communities like the West Indies, the public mind is ever trembling, alive to the dangers of insurrection.[71]

Williams believed that the situation of the British West Indies in 1833 was the climax to three centuries of slave revolts in the Caribbean. 'The emancipation of the slaves in French Saint-Domingue, and their establishment of the independent republic of Haiti, recognized by the Great Powers, elevated the slave revolt from the field of island politics to the sphere of national policy and international diplomacy.' There was a restive spirit in all the Caribbean possession of the British Empire. These revolts had occurred in nearly all territories, but Jamaica was most persistent, with a record of several rebellions. As stated previously, Williams says that the planters blamed the abolitionists for disorder and attributed the ferment among the slaves to the discussion in parliaments.[72]

The slaves, as the governor of Trinidad wrote in 1831, had an unaccountable facility for obtaining partial and generally distorted information whenever a public document was about to be received, which could in any way affect their condition or station. Williams says that they were asking all over the West Indies, 'Why *backra* no do that king bid him?'[73]

International and Intercolonial Rivalry Impacting the Caribbean Slave System

The changing profile of capitalism imposes a constant need upon the nation of Great Britain to re-evaluate its noticeable interest and to develop necessary strategies to remain the leading world power. The advance of capitalism combined with technological transformation had made Great Britain the leading manufacturing country in the world. Capitalism demands markets in order to thrive. However, navigational laws, and monopolies within the British Empire, created strong restrictions upon the potential reach of the British economy. The continued resistance of slaves in the Caribbean, the declining profits of the planters and the over-production of sugar in Brazil, Cuba and India, the new territories, Trinidad and Guiana, created new pressures in the British economy.

Concluding Summary

To summarize the points of this presentation I will outline reflections on Sam Sharpe's life experiences in the context of a cattle slave in the Caribbean slave system. It is evident that western civilization has shaped and fashioned our world during the last 500 years, politically, in religious beliefs, economically, culturally, technologically, in military machinery and security strategies. Although western civilization strived for the assertiveness of the inalienable rights of man, these rights were not extended to the humanity of the African Negro. The slave code of 1661 designated African slaves to be essentially property, and the Caribbean slave system became an economic engine for building capitalism in western civilization. Thus, the ascendency and the dominance of European culture and civilization created a human superiority complex that caused Europeans to believe that they stood highest in the rank of humanity.

In the midst of the oppressive behaviour of systemic racism we must consider that there was also a reformation process that spoke truth to power in parliament and other institutions. While acknowledging the conflicting contributions and undeniable complicity of the European church in the oppression of African peoples, when we consider the oppressive system theologically, we have seen that there is a parallelism that can be found between the oppressed African peoples and biblical figures (and events):

- Historically, it has been established that slaves were sold by their brothers.
- Slaves were subjected to inhuman treatment.
- Slaves were executed by their imperial power.
- Sam Sharpe's execution was a catalyst for the liberation and ultimate freedom of the slaves.
- His sacrifice became an inspiration for building a nation (Jamaica).
- Sam Sharpe became an iconic figure, a metaphor for resistance against the imperial power, as weak and ineffective as it may have seemed.

European civilization has created a crossroads for humanity, a space for the interchange of visions and values for human enrichment. Orlando Costas describes the intersection of exchange as a 'theology of the crossroads' or a critical reflection at the point where cultures, ideologies, religious traditions, and social, economic and political systems confront each other and where the gospel seeks to cross the frontier of unbelief.[74] The theology at the crossroads gives us the analytical tools to deal with our realities as we experience them, according to the context of our lives.

Notes

1 Huntington, Samuel P. (1996), *Clash of Civilizations and the Remaking of World Order*, London: Simon and Schuster.

2 Rousseau, Jean-Jacques (2017), *The Social Contract*, London: Arcturus Publishing, ch. 1.

3 Cranston, Maurice (1999), *The Noble Savage: Jean-Jacques Rousseau, 1754–1762*, Chicago, IL: University of Chicago Press, p. 303.

4 Paine, Thomas (1999), *The Rights of Man*, New York: Dover Publications, p. xvi.

5 Hobson, Theo (2017), *God Created Humanism: The Christian Basis of Secular Values*, London: SPCK, p. 38.

6 Hobson, *God Created Humanism*, p.18.

7 Bronowski, Jacob (2011), *The Ascent Of Man*, London: BBC Books, p. 197.

8 González, Justo L. (2014), *The Story of Christianity: Volume 1: The Early Church to the Dawn of the Reformation*, New York: HarperOne.

9 Huntington, Samuel P. (2004), *Who Are We? The Challenges to America's National Identity*, New York: Simon and Schuster, p. 55.

10 Ferguson, Niall (2012), *Civilization: The West and the Rest*, London: Penguin, p. 129.

11 Ferguson, *Civilization*, p. 129.

12 Ferguson, *Civilization*, p. 129.

13 Roberts, J. M. (2001), *The Triumph of the West*, London: Phoenix Press, p. 14.

14 Fischer, Sibylle (2004), *Modernity Disavowed: Haiti and the Cultures of Slavery in the Age of Revolution*, Durham, NC, and London: Duke University Press, p. 22.

15 Reid-Salmon, Delroy A. (2012), *Burning for Freedom: A Theology of the Black Atlantic Struggle for Liberation*, Kingston: Ian Randle Publishers, p. 41.

16 Kennedy, Fred (2008), *Daddy Sharpe: A Narrative of the Life and Adventures of Samuel Sharpe, a West Indian Slave, Written by Himself, 1832*, Kingston: Ian Randle Publishers, p. 3.

17 Williams, Eric (1994), *Capitalism and Slavery*, Chapel Hill, NC: University of North Carolina Press, p. 20.

18 Williams, *Capitalism and Slavery*, p. 19.

19 Williams, *Capitalism and Slavery*, p. 19.

20 Beckles, Hilary McDonald (2016), *The First Black Slave Society: Britain's 'Barbarity Time' in Barbados, 1636–1876*, Mona: University of the West Indies Press, p. xii.

21 Hall, Catherine, Draper, Nicholas, et al. (2014), *Legacies of British Slave-ownership: Colonial Slavery and the Formation of Victorian Britain*, Cambridge: Cambridge University Press.

22 Williams, Eric (1984), *From Columbus to Castro: The History of the Caribbean 1492–1969*, New York: Vintage Books, p. 30.

23 Ferguson, *Civilization*, p. 105.

24 Ferguson, *Civilization*, p. 105.

25 Sherlock, Sir Phillip Manderson, and Bennett, Hazel (1998), *The Story of the Jamaican People*, Kingston: Ian Randle Publishers, p. 192.

26 Pakenham, Thomas (2015), *The Scramble for Africa*, London: Little, Brown Book Group, p. xxiv.

27 Williams, *Capitalism and Slavery*, p. 7.

28 Williams, *Capitalism and Slavery*, pp. 30, 31.

29 Williams, *Capitalism and Slavery*, p. 52.

30 Williams, *Capitalism and Slavery*, p. 52.

31 Williams, *Capitalism and Slavery*, p. 53.

32 Williams, *From Columbus to Castro*, pp. 280–1.

33 Pakenham, *The Scramble for Africa*, p. xxiv.

34 Pakenham, *The Scramble for Africa*, p. xxiv.

35 Pakenham, *The Scramble for Africa*, p. xxiv.

36 Williams, *Capitalism and Slavery*, p. 98.

37 Williams, *Capitalism and Slavery*, p. 99.

38 Williams, *Capitalism and Slavery*, pp. 99, 100.

39 Williams, *Capitalism and Slavery*, p. 101.

40 Williams, *Capitalism and Slavery*, p. 104.

41 Williams, *Capitalism and Slavery*, p. 105.

42 Williams, *Capitalism and Slavery*, p. 106.

43 Rousseau, *The Social Contract*.

44 Sherlock and Bennett, *The Story of the Jamaican People*, p. 200.

45 Sherlock and Bennett, *The Story of the Jamaican People*, p. 80.

46 Sherlock and Bennett, *The Story of the Jamaican People*, p. 81.

47 Williams, *From Columbus to Castro*, p. 195.

48 Williams, *From Columbus to Castro*, p. 198.

49 A term of West African origin used by Africans and Caribbeans to refer to the white master or white people in general.

50 Sherlock and Bennett, *The Story of the Jamaican People*, p. 200.

51 Sherlock and Bennett, *The Story of the Jamaican People*, pp. 200, 201.

52 Sherlock and Bennett, *The Story of the Jamaican People*, p. 203.

53 Sherlock and Bennett, *The Story of the Jamaican People*, pp. 195, 196.

54 Sherlock and Bennett, *The Story of the Jamaican People*, p. 22.

55 Sherlock and Bennett, *The Story of the Jamaican People*, p. 212.

56 Sherlock and Bennett, *The Story of the Jamaican People*, p. 212.

57 Brathwaite, Kamau (1971), *Development of Creole Society in Jamaica, 1770–1820*, Kingston: Ian Randle Publishers.

58 Sherlock and Bennett, *The Story of the Jamaican People*, p. 212.

59 Brathwaite, *Development of Creole Society in Jamaica*.

60 Sherlock and Bennett, *The Story of the Jamaican People*, p. 213.

61 Williams, *From Columbus to Castro*, p. 292.

62 Williams, *From Columbus to Castro*, p. 293.

63 Williams, *From Columbus to Castro*, p. 293.

64 Howse, Ernest Marshall (1971), *Saints in Politics: The 'Clapham Sect' and the Growth of Freedom*, London: Allen and Unwin, p. 15.

65 Williams, *From Columbus to Castro*, p. 295.

66 Williams, *From Columbus to Castro*, p. 293.

67 Williams, *From Columbus to Castro*, p. 296.

68 Williams, *From Columbus to Castro*, p. 304.

69 Williams, *From Columbus to Castro*, p. 305.

70 Williams, *From Columbus to Castro*, p. 310.

71 Williams, *From Columbus to Castro*, p. 321.

72 Williams, *From Columbus to Castro*, p. 323.

73 Williams, *From Columbus to Castro*, p. 323.

74 Costas, Orlando E. (1976), *Theology of the Crossroads in Contemporary Latin America: Missiology in Mainline Protestatism 1969–1974*, Amsterdam: Rodopi.

4

Women in Sam Sharpe's Army: Repression, Resistance, Reparation

Professor Verene A. Shepherd, 2019

This is Heritage Month in Jamaica (when we honour national heroes and recall the Morant Bay War of 1865 in which, at the order of the Bedfordshire-born Governor John Eyre, over 400 Black people were murdered); and it is Black History Month here in the UK. I will not enter the debate about whether or not they are necessary. They exist now, and so in the spirit of Black History and Heritage Month, I pay tribute to all our ancestors in Africa who created great civilizations and empowered us to know that our history did not start with slavery; the men and women on both sides of the Atlantic, enslaved and free, who fought against capture and enslavement; who employed diverse strategies to agitate for the ending of what was arguably the greatest crime against humanity; who in the post-slavery and post-independence periods continued the fight for justice; the Black men and women whose blood, sweat and tears built this country so that when we see the so-called 'great houses' and castles (to which we should have free access for life, by the way); the banks and insurance companies, the churches and universities on this landscape, we can say: our ancestors made them possible; men and women who in the post-colonial period, like the Windrush generation and their descendants, continued the struggle for rights and respect. May we never dishonour them by giving up the fight against injustice grounded in racial discrimination.

I pay respects to my own enslaved ancestor, Alexander Mighty, my great, great grandfather, who was born into slavery in Jamaica in 1829 but was left at five years old at the time of emancipation in 1834 with nothing but freedom, unlike the planter class who received compensation. I speak this evening on behalf of all the ancestors who lost their lives in the anti-colonial liberation movements in Jamaica because they had to finish what the Tainos, the Maroons, Chief Takyi, Sam Sharpe and others had started. So let us invite their spirits to occupy the spaces around us as we seek the appeasement of their torture and the redemption of their souls.

I hope that at the end of this evening's deliberations, we will all agree that the denial of reparation for the wrongs of the past is abhorrent to the spirit of justice and intensify our resolve to demand reparation from those who wronged our ancestors but who have to date refused to take responsibility for that wrong or engage in a reparatory justice conversation.

Among those who bore the brunt of British terrorism in the Caribbean were enslaved women who had no choice but to resist the repression of African enslavement, many of whom must be regarded as soldiers in Sam Sharpe's army and abolitionists in the cause of emancipation.

I know that we are more accustomed to viewing as abolitionists men like Mansfield, Fox, Wilberforce, Clarkson, Knibb and Newton and women like Queen Victoria, Anne Knight (Quaker, Essex), Mary Birkett Card; Georgina, the Duchess of Devonshire, and Elizabeth Heyrick. But thanks to those like Lucille Mathurin Mair, who, since the emergence of the definable field of women's history, have used their scholarship in the service of knowledge production so that we now know what others never wanted us to know, we can confidently extend the term 'abolitionists' to the women and men on the plantations, who destabilized systems of colonial domination.

The revisionist historians have brought the history of the Black abolitionist women in Sharpe's army to our attention. Their formidable analyses represent powerful counter-discourses to the type of knowledge production that marginalized women's fundamental role in capital accumulation and the destabilization of the slave system, and they bring truth to the African proverb, 'Until the lion tells his own story, the tale of the hunt will glorify the hunter.' That also applies to the Lioness!

Repression

Who were some of these women who supported Samuel Sharpe, the acknowledged leader of the 1831/32 Emancipation War in Jamaica, which started in St James but practically engulfed the whole island? A man born in 1801 and hanged for his activism on 23 May 1832, aged 31; a native Baptist preacher whose anti-slavery commitment made him take up arms – a fowling piece reportedly – and made his lieutenants swear an oath on the Christian Bible to fight for freedom when peaceful protest seemed unworkable. And, by the way, when I read the eyewitness account that Sharpe had a fowling piece, I thought he had a hen coop or kept chickens until someone told me it was a shotgun or scattergun. With suitable reverence, I call their names:

Catherine Brown	Enslaved by Mrs Griffiths, Coventry Estate	Hanover Parish
Catherine Clarke	Enslaved by Dr W. Skirving, Woodlands Estate	Hanover Parish
Ann James	A Free woman from Hanover Parish who apparently joined the rebels	
Christina James	Enslaved by Mrs Griffiths, Coventry Estate	Hanover Parish
Eliza James	Enslaved by Mrs Griffiths, Coventry Estate	Hanover Parish
Susan James	Enslaved by Mrs Griffiths, Coventry Estate	Hanover Parish
Ann Ramsay	Beans Estate	Hanover Parish
Mary Campbell	Not stated	St Elizabeth Parish

| Nancy Campbell | Ipswich Estate | St Elizabeth Parish |
| Sarah Darling | Mitcham Estate | St Elizabeth Parish |

It was the very existence of slavery that caused these women to engage in acts of resistance. Once located in the Americas, they were enslaved in large numbers and subjected to various forms of exploitation and control, not least those categorized as property and unfree labourers, and forced to work without wages, mainly in fields, factories and planters' houses. Enslavers appropriated their reproductive lives by claiming their children as property and used skin colour as justification for making women reproduce the status of enslavement, unlike white women who could only reproduce free status, even if Black men fathered their children.[1] They were subjected to rape, or 'sexploitation'; for neither colonial statutes nor codes, which formed a part of the superstructure of slavery designed to control those enslaved, invested enslaved women with any rights over their own bodies, but, rather, transferred and consolidated such rights within the legal person of the enslavers.[2] Laws also sought to defeminize women, and race became a crucial factor in the social stratification of the slave societies[3] and heightened the struggle for rights and equality in the entire Caribbean.[4]

Resistance

Every form of control generates an opposing struggle for liberation. As Harriet Jacobs said, 'My master had power and law on his side; I had a determined will. There is might in each.' Gendered patterns of resistance emerged in attempts to enforce white supremacy through racialized slavery. Modern scholarship affirms that Black women were a fundamental part of the campaign for freedom and rights in the colonial Caribbean and that anti-slavery activism was not the preserve of males (as was argued by the older scholarship). Many eighteenth- and nineteenth-century accounts testify to enslaved women's rebelliousness and resistance to rape and to the plantation work regime. Bernard Senior, a British military officer active in the suppression of the 1831/32 anti-slavery war in Jamaica led by Sam Sharpe, in describing instances of malingering, insolence and the attempt to enforce moral economy on several plantations, admitted that 'women, as well as men, were alike defaulters'.[5] They participated in armed revolt, marronage and in the day-to-day acts of resistance that destabilized the regime on which slavery rested. It was Frederick Douglas who said, 'When the true history of the antislavery cause shall be written, women will occupy a large space in its pages; for the cause of the slave has been peculiarly woman's cause.'[6]

The storyboard at Kensington in the parish of St James where the 1831/32 Emancipation War started states boldly that an enslaved woman, eventually executed by the soldiers for her action after lighting the first flames, is reported to have said, 'I know I shall die for it, but my children shall be free!'[7] Minister Grange has christened her Fire!

Bernard Senior tells us that a party of soldiers, tracking down rebels who had taken 15 white women captive, captured a young Black woman who had abandoned her task of filling five gourds with water when she heard them approaching. According to Senior, the enslaved woman 'pretended great penitence, acknowledging that she had long ago left her owner's service, without leave or cause, but (having been out so long) denied any knowledge of the insurrection'.[8] She did admit that she had heard that, as soon as the Baptist parson returned from England, all the enslaved would be free. But she left the plantation because she thought there would be no harm in taking her freedom a little before the time appointed.[9] Asked why one person needed so much water, she said that she was living in the woods by herself and that on the day in question she was washing all her clothes and wished to carry plenty of water at once for the purpose. One of the soldiers decided she was lying and commanded her to lead them to where the rebels were keeping the captives. She proceeded to do just that – or so the soldiers thought. She was, in fact, leading them away from the camp. But unfortunately for her, this was soon discovered; for one of the soldiers noticed that she carefully avoided every heavily travelled path and invariably took those newly cut and little-used ones. After going 100 yards or so past a path with its entrance blocked with newly cut logwood branches (which the woman had passed without so much as a glance), one of the soldiers insisted that he had heard voices at a little distance in the woods.

According to Senior:

> She affirmed that it was quite impossible, as she knew every track in the neighbourhood, and the logwood had been cut by herself and placed there to prevent stray cattle from destroying her small provision ground, which they had latterly been in the habit of doing.[10]

The soldiers proceeded for a short distance further but eventually became suspicious and decided to go back and explore the barricaded path that they had passed. They also confronted the woman, accusing her of lying, and held a gun to her head to force her to confess. She immediately fell on her knees, acknowledged that she belonged to a strong party of well-armed rebels and that what she had been doing was conducting them to the rebel retreat. She was confident that such a small group of white soldiers would have been easily killed by the rebels before they could retreat. At that precise moment of discovery, the soldiers were within a quarter of a mile of the rebels. She also admitted that the barricaded entrance led to the place where 15 white women were being held hostage.[11]

Women provided motivation for the soldiers. The following were among women's roles: pre-combat ancestral rituals, strategic manoeuvring, supplying water, acting as guides to provision grounds, helping to guard captives, poisoning, and acting as lookouts and even as go-betweens in the final stage of rebellions. Women cooked food for the bands of rebels who stopped at various properties for revictualling purposes. They were one with the cause, as articulated by William Binham:

> The Baptists all believe that they are to be freed; they say the Lord and the King have given them free, but the white gentlemen in Jamaica keep it back; they said if they did not fight for freedom, they would never get it. I heard them all say this.[12]

Repression

Women suffered for their activism, as the punishment list in the UK National Archives indicates. For instance, Eliza Whittingham, Jane Whittingham, Catherine Brown and Christina James were sentenced to death. Susanna James got 200 lashes; Eliza James, Caroline Smith and Ann Ramsay got 100 lashes; and Sarah Jackson and Priscilla were transported out of the island for life.

These punishments make for chilling reading, but they are tangible reminders that our ancestors never accepted enslavement uncomplainingly. Monuments, like the one built in Montego Bay in 2007, symbolize our collective debt to them. Governor Belmore was quite aware that the punishments for many were out of proportion to the so-called 'crimes' committed, but he defended the horrendous punishments ordered thus:

> I regret to state, that in suppressing this most calamitous rebellion, many slaves have perished in the field, and numbers have been executed after trial, but the audacity of the rebels was so great, that striking examples were found indispensably necessary, for mistaken lenity [leniency] would have only operated as an indirect encouragement to the disaffected to persevere in their lawless designs.[13]

Memories of these killings, centuries after the introduction of the slavery system to the Caribbean, cause what Edward Linenthal describes as that 'indigestible fishbone of slavery' to continue to stick in our throats.[14]

If you are tempted to ask, after being introduced to these women, 'Where on earth did such women, the alleged "subordinate sex", get the nerve [to confront systems of domination]?' Lucille Mair's answer? 'It came from their very subordination – the moral force of the powerless confronting the powerful – and from their ability to draw strength from that inheritance of ancestral spirits from that other side of the ocean.'[15]

Reparation

It is for these enslaved women that I urge us to be intentional in support of the cause of reparatory justice and engage in public education so that an informed citizenry can force former colonizers to meet their demands. Reparation rests on moral, legal and political grounds, and the reparation demand is not only for native genocide and African enslavement but also for deceptive indentureship and post-colonial harm. Indeed, the legacies of these atrocities have contributed to continued Caribbean underdevelopment.

We need to admit that close to 180 years after emancipation in 1838, the people of the Caribbean are still struggling to achieve true political and economic independence and sustainable development, end poverty and make the region less vulnerable to the ravages of natural and man-made disasters and the impact of climate change and centuries-old environmental degradation. While a multiplicity of strategies have been pursued by the Caribbean in its efforts to overcome socio-economic, environmental and political challenges, especially after gaining independence from Western European Powers, as those powers left the region un- and underdeveloped after having used our resources, with indigenous and forcefully imported labour, to ensure its own development, reparation as part of decolonial justice for such underdevelopment has been placed on the table. Reparation also seeks to address continuing harm, seen most vividly in the expressions of racism that still affect so many of us globally.

Indeed, despite the independence, emancipation, post-emancipation, civil rights and more modern struggles against colonialism, anti-Black racism, Afro-phobia and other forms of injustice, inequality and discrimination still attach themselves parasitically to people of African descent all over the world. The circle of racism still threatens to choke us, as the slave collar did our enslaved ancestors. In the post-emancipation Caribbean, a century or more of racial apartheid impeded our actualization of our freedom because the colonizers were never committed to emancipation. After all, the financial settlement that accompanied it cemented the British attitude that our ancestors were property. Today, we may have political independence, but neo-colonialism is squeezing our throats so tightly that, at times, we, too, can't breathe. African people are still walking in a circle, so vividly represented in the 2015 Man Booker prize winner Marlon James' historical novel *The Book of Night Women*: 'Every Negro walks in a circle. Take that and make of it what you will. A circle like a sun, a circle like a moon, a circle like bad tidings that seem gone but always come back.'[16]

What many have described as the immorality, political irresponsibility and social injustice of European colonizers who conceived of, capitalized, managed and benefited from the Ma'angamizi or African holocaust for over 400 years form the philosophical underpinnings of the movement for reparatory justice in the Caribbean. The policy and practice of reparatory justice have been features of European/American jurisprudence and history for over two centuries. It has always been conceived of as a way to redress wrongs, current or historic, achieve peace and reconciliation, and clear precedent exists.

The pioneers of the reparation movement were enslaved Africans all over the Caribbean who knew their illegal entrapment in Babylon was a violation of their human rights and struggled to end the transatlantic trade in enslaved Africans and enslavement. In the immediate post-slavery period, the newly emancipated took up the struggle, enforcing ideas of moral economy in their efforts to secure land and decent wages for decent work. Randall Robinson, in his path-breaking book *The Debt: What America Owes to Blacks*, tells us that formerly enslaved people themselves long recognized reparation's potential to right historical wrongs, including in his book this extract from Jourdon Anderson's 7 August 1865 letter to his former enslaver. Jourdon, once in Big Spring, Tennessee, told his former enslaver that before he would consider returning to his employ as he had written to request, a just financial settlement was necessary:

Sir ... if you will write and say what wages you will give me, I will be better able to decide whether it would be to my advantage to move back again ... and we have concluded to test your sincerity by asking you to send us your wages for the time we served you. I have served you faithfully for 32 years, and [my wife] Mandy, 20 years. At 25 dollars a month for me and two dollars a week for Mandy, our earnings would amount to eleven thousand six hundred and eighty dollars. Add to this the interest for the time our wages have been kept back, and deduct what you paid for our clothing, and three doctor's visits to me, and pulling a tooth for Mandy, and the balance will show what we are in justice entitled to ... Please send the money by Adam's Express.[17]

The eighteenth- and nineteenth-century enslaved-led wars all over the Caribbean, the Morant Bay War in Jamaica and the 1930s labour protests across the Caribbean all continued this search for reparatory justice as the governing classes sought either to maintain slavery or recreate the mentalities and practices of slavery in the post-slavery period, and the masses refused to cooperate in their project.

The post-1930s advocates for freedom, democracy and reparatory justice were the Rastafari, whose claim was for African redemption and repatriation. They have since been joined by NGOs, academics, civil society and individual politicians on all sides of the Atlantic and, since 2013, by the governments of CARICOM, who have articulated, as a negotiating strategy, a Ten Point Action Plan.

Before setting out the plan, I admit that the Durban Declaration and Programme of Action (DDPA) and the Programme of Action (POA) for the Decade have suggested solutions for how states can address the crisis of underdevelopment in post-colonial societies. But those solutions are rather vague and non-binding and are framed within the context of what David Martin terms 'lexical colonialism',[18] with insufficient emphasis placed on the recipient and not enough empowerment of the 'recipient' to deal with the 'artefact being transferred'.[19]

The 10 Point Action Plan – which I know is not universally supported – begins with a restatement of the rationale for the reparation movement in the region, with the CARICOM

Reparations Commission (CRC) asserting that the region's indigenous and African descendant communities who are the victims of crimes against humanity in the forms of genocide, enslavement, human trafficking and racial apartheid have a legal right to reparatory justice, and that those who committed these crimes, and who have been enriched by the proceeds of these crimes, have a reparatory case to answer. The plan recognizes the special role and status of European governments in this regard, being the legal bodies that instituted the framework for developing and sustaining these crimes and served as the primary agencies through which slavery-based enrichment took place and as national custodians of criminally accumulated wealth.

The CRC then sets out the charges against the transgressors and elaborates on the strategy for reparatory justice:

1 Full formal apology.
2 An Indigenous Peoples Development Programme.
3 Repatriation for those who desire it.
4 The establishment of cultural institutions.
5 Addressing the public health crisis.
6 Illiteracy eradication
7 The development of an African Knowledge Programme.
8 Psychological rehabilitation.
9 Technology transfer, which can be located within the right-to-development framework.

The right-to-development focus is not only captured in the works of scholars who established for us the roots of Caribbean underdevelopment but also in the artistic expressions of our artistes. In a verse from 'Slave Driver',[20] the Honourable Robert Nesta 'Bob' Marley wailed: 'Every time I hear the crack of the whip', evoking a collective memory of the slave ship.

Marley's song not only reflects the memories of ancestral suffering via the transatlantic trade in enslaved Africans but the lines 'today they say we are free; only to be chained in poverty' could very well have been commissioned by the CARICOM Reparations Commission. The Programme of Activities of the

Decade for People of African Descent, grounded in the Durban Declaration and Programme of Action, emphasizes the need for apology, repair and reconciliation as a way of closing the dark chapters in our history.

10 Finally, the Caribbean reparatory Justice Programme includes debt cancellation and monetary compensation – on the basis that the Caribbean governments that emerged from slavery and colonialism have inherited the massive crisis of community poverty and institutional unpreparedness for development.[21]

The post-independence demand for development with input from former colonial powers still continues, especially as nationalist leaders, anxious to capitalize on the 'prostrate condition of European nations after World War II',[22] in Bruce Seely's words, never pressed for compensation. On the contrary, the new nations, founded with much hope, faced daunting economic challenges. Seely quotes Ahmad and Wilkie, who noted: 'These nations soon began to realize that political freedom could not be construed as an end in itself and that achieving it did not automatically ensure the social and economic well-being of their people.'[23] The pressure of development has driven governments to carry the burden of public employment and social policies designed to confront colonial legacies.

Reparation advocates use other reasons as justification:

- The injustice is well documented.
- Plantation slavery provided the scaffold for Britain's industrial advancement.
- A defendant (or perpetrator) exists.
- The victims are identifiable as a distinct group.
- The descendants of victimized groups continue to suffer harm. This remains true today as the institutionalized racism of the colonial era has had a debilitating impact on Africans and people of African descent. Colonialism has economically disenfranchised Africans and people of African descent.

- There is precedent for the payment of reparation (Ayiti, Jews, British planters).
- The right to reparation is recognized by international law.

It is supported by Clause 158 of the DDPA, which recognizes that

> Historical injustices have undeniably contributed to the poverty, underdevelopment, marginalization, social exclusion, economic disparities, instability and insecurity that affect many people in different parts of the world, in particular in developing countries; and recognizes the need to develop programmes for the social and economic development of these societies and the Diaspora, within the framework of a new partnership based on the spirit of solidarity and mutual respect.[24]

Royal families throughout Europe developed financial interests in the trade, and slavery was profitable for the British economy. One should recall that the English gave royal patronage to the Transatlantic Trade in enslaved Africans (TTA) and slavery through the establishment of the Company of Royal Adventurers Trading to Africa, which, after five years of operation, was recapitalized and incorporated into the Royal African Company (RAC) in 1663. The RAC was chaired by the Duke of York, a nephew to the then King, and members of the royal family were prominent investors in it. This is a reason for involving the present monarchy in the reparation claim, as the royal family inherited wealth from that period.

In March 2007, British MP Diane Abbott reminded her parliamentary colleagues that 15 Lord Mayors, 25 sheriffs and 38 aldermen were shareholders in the RAC. It is estimated that, in 1776, 40 members of the British parliament were making their money from investments in the Caribbean. *Compensation was paid to the enslavers and their beneficiaries.*

Let me hasten to say, though, that the rightness of the reparation struggle is not self-evident to all, and even if the right to reparation is recognized by international law, as outlined by the Permanent Court of International Justice (PCIJ), the predecessor of the International Court of Justice (ICJ) in its *Factory at Chorzów (Merits)* decision, opposition abounds, using the following arguments:

- Too long ago, in the past.
- There are no victims/they are all dead.
- Descendants cannot claim on behalf of their ancestors.
- The majority of Caribbean people are not in favour of the movement.
- Caribbean people are opposed to repatriation.
- It was Africans who sold our ancestors.
- Too complicated a matter.
- Governments cannot pay.

One or the other or a combination of these views have been carried by Jamaicans like Lipton Matthews, by former UK prime ministers and functionaries from Blair and Cameron to the current UK High Commissioner in Jamaica, Asif Ahmad – all aimed at detaching the modern legacies of chattel enslavement and redirecting it to modern human trafficking and other current human rights issues. The leader of the Labour Party disagrees, I see.

From all accounts, Britain's posture is not new where the Caribbean is concerned, for history has shown that Britain has not always lived up to its responsibilities. For example, Britain was anxious, as Gordon K. Lewis reminds us in *The Growth of the Modern West Indies*, to use federation as a means of discarding its, then unwanted, responsibilities as a colonial power.[25] In his words, Britain 'sought withdrawal from the Caribbean area without providing the sort of economic aid to which, on any showing, the colonies were entitled'. Sir Ellis Clarke, who was the Trinidadian government's UN representative to a subcommittee of the Committee on Colonialism in 1964, had made this point in his statement:

'An administering power ... is not entitled to extract for centuries all that can be got out of a colony and when that has been done to relieve itself of its obligations by the conferment of a formal but meaningless – meaningless because it cannot possibly be supported – political independence.

Justice requires that reparation be made to the country that has suffered the ravages of colonialism before that country is expected to face up to the problems and difficulties that will inevitably beset it upon independence.' ... 'Anything less than that ...', Sir Ellis Clarke concluded, 'would constitute something less than the genuine article; it would be trying to fob off West Indians with independence on the cheap.' He went on to suggest that Britain was not facing up to its moral and financial obligations.[26]

But there is growing support, although the energy unleashed by cartoonists and politicians like the Most Hon. P. J. Patterson ebbs and flows. Still, while the former colonial powers have failed to go beyond statements of regret, some educational institutions (e.g. Georgetown, Glasgow, Brown, Emory, Dalhousie) and churches (the Jamaica Baptist Union, the Southern Baptists (1985), the Jesuit Order, The Episcopal Church, the Council of World Missions linked to the London Missionary Society, the World Council of Churches, World Communion of Reformed Churches and the Lutheran World Federation) have apologized or taken on acts of reparation. Indeed, the former colonial powers have dug in their heels, evidenced by the negative responses to CARICOM's letter of demand to six of them. Former French President Hollande, for example, stated that history cannot be erased. We do not erase it. It cannot be the subject of transactions at the end of an accounting exercise which would be, at all points, impossible to establish. This is ironic because emancipation was made an accounting exercise when the British compensated the enslavers.

While complicit nations stall, anti-Black racism is escalating around the world. We have seen it in the treatment of migrants; we have seen it in racial profiling in various societies and at national borders. Each day we see reports about racial acts on our TV screens, via social media or over the airwaves. We all know about the cases of Stephen Lawrence, Mark Duggan, Trayvon Martin, Jordan Davis, Michael Brown, Eric Garner, and so many more highlighted here in the UK and in the Black Lives Matter Movement in the USA.

So why does the movement for reparatory justice still occupy the energies of so many people, especially within the culture of disunity and the presence of vocal anti-reparationists? Can we really destabilize white supremacy, which many see as the obstacle to reparatory justice? Is Nell Painter right when she asserts that the racial 'idea of Blackness' would likely always be with us, meaning also that white supremacy will always be with us? How do we sit with the idea that, as Ta-Nehisi Coates observes, while the Black political tradition is essentially hopeful, history shows us too many examples of heroic people whose struggles were not successful in their own time or at all? On the contrary, to the extent that they were successful, Black politics was a necessary precondition but never enough to foment change.

Coates admits that not even emancipation should be viewed as a triumph of Black activism or the moral force of the actions of the just over the unjust. He holds that,

> It became impossible, for instance, to think about emancipation without the threat presented by disunion, to talk about the civil-rights movement without the ghost of Nazism or the Cold War. It began to seem to me that Black politics was the wind at the American window. At rare moments the window opened, and Black people pushed through. The window seemed to open for one reason and one reason alone – some threat to white interests becoming intolerable.

In this formulation, it is not enough to be hopeful that good will triumph over evil because '"Hope" [might be] an overrated force in human history – unlike fear.'[27]

So, what will be the wind at the American and Caribbean window that will open up and create fear among former colonizers to enable the cause of reparatory justice to push through, especially in the face of the tenacity of white supremacy and the tenacity of injustice?

I do not have the answer. All I know is that ahistorical as it may seem to some, we in the reparation movement have decided not to live in hopelessness. We wish to use the sections of the programme of activities for the International Decade for

People of African Descent, which speak to reparatory justice and reconciliation, to hold States to their obligations. But we who believe in freedom cannot rest until it comes.

Reparation is a right to redress and repair, not an act of begging. Perhaps José Marti sums it up best: 'Rights are to be taken, not requested; seized, not begged for.'[28] As Doudou Diene, Senegalese Director of Inter-Cultural Projects, said in 2004 at a function to mark the Haitian bicentenary, 'The fight for human rights is a fight for remembrance, for any tragedy hidden away can appear again in different forms.'

Bob Marley and HIM Haile Selassie I put it another way, framing their ideas within the context of white supremacy:

Until the philosophy which holds one race superior and another inferior is finally and permanently discredited and abandoned, everywhere is war. Until there are no longer first-class and second-class citizens of any nation; until the colour of a person's skin is of no more significance than the colour of his/her eyes; until the basic human rights are equally guaranteed to all, without regard to race – Dis a war. That until that day, the dream of lasting peace, world citizenship and rule of international morality will remain but a fleeting illusion to be pursued, but never attained.[29]

War is not what we need, but the wind at the American and Caribbean window that will open up and create fear among former colonizers to enable the cause of reparatory justice to push through, especially in the face of the tenacity of white supremacy and the tenacity of injustice.

Conclusion

I have taken you through a journey of activism and agency of our foremothers. Activism and agency are particularly relevant when speaking about ex-colonial societies where issues of freedom, human rights, restorative justice, citizenship and self-determination had to be settled by rebel men and women before the issues of feminism and women's rights could form a part of the national anti-colonial discourse. Indeed, modern-day women's movements and feminism cannot be understood without excavating and locating the prior waves of activism and theorizing on women's conditions dating back centuries. Long before the year 1851, at the Women's Convention in Akron, Ohio, where Sojourner Truth asked, 'Ain't I a woman' and spoke the truth about women's rights;[30] 8 March 1857, in New York, when garment workers protested inhumane working conditions (and later gave inspiration for International Women's Day); and 1977 when UNESCO proclaimed International Women's Day, rebel women in the African Atlantic used a variety of strategies to eradicate, or at least destabilize and subvert, systems of domination. Anti-slavery, in fact, helped the feminist movement. Free women saw in slavery parallels to their own oppressed conditions based on gender, and developed, out of this perception, arguments for female emancipation.

All that is left for us to do is sing praise songs to them and seek redress for what they did for our liberation. The fight against historical injustices is as important as the fight against current ones, especially as there is a link between the past and the present. In their honour, I ask that you rise and join me as we call their names and keep them in our hearts and be proud that we, their descendants, are alive to argue their cause in the interest of justice.

Catherine Brown	Death – commuted to 50 lashes & 6 weeks imprisonment.
Catherine Clarke	50 lashes & 3 months in prison at hard labour
Ann James	Death/executed
Christina James	50 lashes & 3 months in prison at hard labour
Eliza James	100 lashes, 2 months & 50 lashes when discharged
Susan James	200 lashes, 2 months & 50 lashes when discharged

Ann Ramsay	100 lashes, 6 months & 50 lashes when discharged
Mary Campbell	150 lashes
Nancy Campbell	50 lashes
Sarah Darling	15 lashes
Anna Freeburn	50 lashes & 3 months in prison
Sarah Jackson	Transportation for life
Sophia Maitland	25 lashes
Jane Maitland	25 lashes
Matty	50 lashes
Amelia Murray	100 lashes
Betsy Powell	20 lashes
Priscilla	Transportation for life
Jenny	Death
Caroline Smith	100 lashes
Charlotte Smith	50 lashes
Mary Walker	10 lashes
Suzanna Wright	25 lashes
Nancy Wright	20 lashes
Eliza Lawrence	50 lashes & 6 months in prison
Kitty Scarlett	Death/commuted to transportation
Rebecca Grant	100 lashes
Mary Fowler	6 months in prison
Elizabeth Samuels	100 lashes & 6 months in prison
Rosanna alias Annie Steele	3 months in prison
Charlotte Reid	6 months in prison
Eliza Whittingham	Death
Jane Whittingham	Death/hanged

Source: Parliamentary Papers, Jamaica: Slave Trials and Punishment,
1831–32.

May we never betray their memory. An injustice without a remedy is abhorrent to the spirit of justice.
I thank you.

Notes

1 See Beckles, Hilary (1999), 'Property Rights in Pleasure: The Marketing of Black Women's Sexuality', in Hilary Beckles, *Centering Woman: Gender Discourses in Caribbean Slave Society*, Kingston: Ian Randle Publishers, pp. 22–37.

2 Goveia, Elsa (1965), *Slave Society in the British Leeward Islands*, New Haven: Yale University Press, p. 313.

3 Beckles, 'Property Rights in Pleasure', p. 23.

4 Cox, Edward (1984), *Free Coloureds in the Slave Societies of St. Kitts and Grenada*, Knoxville, TN: University of Tennessee Press, p. 34.

5 Senior, Bernard (1835), *Jamaica As It Is, As It Was and As It May Be*, London: T. Hurst, p. 171.

6 See Hall, Douglas (1989), *In Miserable Slavery: Thomas Thistlewood in Jamaica, 1750–1786*, London: Macmillan; and Beckles, Hilary (1999), 'Phibbah's Price', in Beckles, *Centering Woman*, pp. 38–58. See also Shepherd, Verene (2009), *Livestock, Sugar and Slavery: Contested Terrain in Colonial Jamaica*, Kingston: Ian Randle Publishers.

7 See the storyboard at Kensington Estate, St James; see also Conford, Revd P. H. (1895), *Missionary Reminiscences or Jamaica Retraced*, Leeds: J. Heaton & Son, 1895.

8 Senior, *Jamaica*, pp. 214–15.

9 Senior, *Jamaica*, p. 215.

10 Senior, *Jamaica*, p. 216.

11 Senior, *Jamaica*, p. 216.

12 C.O. 137/181. Papers Relating to the Slave Insurrection, Jamaica. 'Confession of William Binham, a prisoner under sentence of death', to Rev. Thomas Stewart and Rev. Daniel Fidler, 19 January 1832, f. 32. See also Jamaica Archives, 21/3 (194), *Votes*, Appendix 18, Enclosure 4, p. 340.

13 Jamaica Archives, *Votes*, 21/3 (194). Address by Governor Belmore, p. 3.

14 Quoted in Linenthal, Edward T. (2006), 'Epilogue: Reflections', in James O. Horton and Lois E. Horton, eds, *Slavery and Public History: The Tough Stuff of American Memory*, New York: The New Press, p. 213.

15 Mair, Lucille Mathurin (2007), 'Recollections into a Journey of a Rebel Past', reproduced as 'Epilogue', in Lucille Mathurin Mair, *A*

Historical Study of Women in Jamaica, 1655–1838, Kingston: The Press, University of the West Indies.

16 James, Marlon (2010), *The Book of Night Women*, New York: Riverhead, p. 32.

17 Robinson, Randall (2000), *The Debt: What America Owes the Blacks*, London: Penguin, p. 241.

18 Martin, David, 'Thoughts on Technology Transfer and Commercialization', Innovation and Entrepreneurship, p. 3.

19 Martin, 'Thoughts', p. 3.

20 Bob Marley and the Wailers, 1973, 'Slave Driver', *Catch a Fire*, Tuff Gong & Island Records.

21 For the CARICOM Ten Point Plan for Reparatory Justice, see https://caricom.org/caricom-ten-point-plan-for-reparatory-justice/ (accessed 5.6.23).

22 Seely, Bruce, April 2003, 'Historical Patterns in the Scholarship of Technology Transfer', *Comparative Technology Transfer & Society* 1, pp. 7–48, p. 11.

23 Ahmad, A. and Wilkie, A. S. (1979), 'Technology Transfer in the New International Economic Order: Options, Obstacles, and Dilemmas', in J. McIntyre and D. S. Papp, eds, *The Political Economy of International Technology Transfer*, New York: Quorum, pp. 77–94.

24 The Durban Declaration and Programme of Action (2002), United Nations Department of Public Information, New York (available at: www.un.org), p. 103.

25 Lewis, Gordon K. (2004), *The Growth of the Modern West Indies*, Kingston: Ian Randle Publishers, p. 385.

26 Lewis, *The Growth of the Modern West Indies*, p. 385.

27 Coates, Ta-Nehisi (2015), 'Hope and the Historian', *The Atlantic*, 10 December, available at: https://www.theatlantic.com/politics/archive/2015/12/hope-and-the-historian/419961/ (accessed 5.6.23).

28 Marti, José (1975), *Inside the Monster: Writings on the United States and American Imperialism*, ed. Philip S. Foner, trans. Elinor Randall, New York: Monthly Review Press, p. 27; Bailey, Anne C. (2006), *African Voices of the Transatlantic Slave Trade: Beyond the Silence and the Shame*, Boston, MA: Beacon Press.

29 Spoken to the United Nations General Assembly on 4 October 1963, and often considered inspiration for Bob Marley and the Wailers' song 'War', 1976.

30 Whalin, W. Terry (1997), *Sojourner Truth: American Abolitionist*. Ohio: Barbour Publishing Inc., p. 129.

5

Members of One Another:
Fleeting Illusion or Faithful Pursuit

Revd Karl Johnson, 2017

One hundred and eighty-five years ago, on 23 May 1832, the man in whose name and memory this lecture is named was hanged in St James, Jamaica. He was murdered by the state for his role in what was viewed as a bloody uprising. For Jamaicans, however, Sam Sharpe is a national hero and universal icon of resistance and courage. His spirit and legacy are alive and inspirational among us today as we remember his conviction to defy the powers of evil, choosing 'rather to die on yonder gallows than live in slavery'! I am deeply honoured, therefore, to be associated with this lecture series and, doubly so, to have been asked to share some thoughts on the occasion of the sixth staging.

It ought to be stated from the outset that being tasked with this assignment is more linked to my office and role as General Secretary of the Jamaica Baptist Union than any alignment of my ability and competence with the stellar list of scholars who have delivered the previous five lectures. Even more so, however, it is linked to the fact that this year marks the tenth anniversary of the Swanwick Apology for Slavery and the Slave Trade offered by British Baptists in November 2007. I have so dubbed it because of where it took place, Swanwick (Derbyshire), in Britain.

A watershed moment by any measure, the apology has led to a kind of renaissance of the relationship between Jamaican and British Baptists, a relationship that was officially forged in 1814 when the first British clergy arrived on 23 February. Additionally, the decision to personally (on a visit, from 22–29

May 2008) deliver the apology on the soil that had soaked up so much of the blood, sweat and tears of our forebears was deemed a positive gesture of sincerity. Allow me to say that our time together following those events has led some of us to believe that the process leading up to, as well as the apology itself, may ultimately have its most lasting impact on the way British Baptists organize themselves for ongoing mission.

In keeping with that viewpoint, this lecture will seek to highlight some perspectives arising from my reflections on our journey thus far. The topic I have chosen, 'Members of One Another: Fleeting Illusion or Faithful Pursuit', is meant to be a divine plumb line against which to reflect on the journey. Based on Romans 12.5, these words of the Apostle Paul set a tone, offer an outlook, and imply an imperative relevant to whether, as church, we are reflecting a particular gospel non-negotiable. The words suggest (within their scope) that the church, in any authentic expression of its life, ought to be an integrated, non-discriminatory community of believers with a shared commitment to Christ Jesus and empowered by the Spirit to serve a common cause. This common cause goes beyond its own self-nurturing but embraces a definitive missional purpose.

Let me say one more thing before proceeding, and that is that I wish for us all to remember that I speak as one whose experience has been shaped by a historical context of the underside or other side of mission, as some would say – that is, a mission-field with all that this implies. I live, move and have my being in a country that knows first-hand the full implications of chattel slavery, an extended period of colonial rule after slavery and a post-colonial existence with continuing legacies of colonialism that remain alive in our memory and continue to be a shaping influence in our daily life.

Introduction

I remember exactly where I was when I received news of the historic Swanwick Apology. I was in Trinidad and Tobago, participating in a week of revival meetings when David Kerrigan, then Director of International Mission at the Baptist Missionary Society, sent me an email sharing what had happened. Perhaps if it were today, I would have dismissed it as fake news, but what I can say is that several feelings gripped me as I read that email. There were feelings of relief, joy, disappointment, anger and scepticism – I could go on and on.

The Swanwick Apology was offered a little under five months after some Jamaicans, along with other members of the worldwide Baptist family, gathered for a Service of Memory and Reconciliation at the Elmira Slave Castle in Accra, Ghana and witnessed members of the Baptist Union of Great Britain (BUGB) contingent refuse to join with others in apologizing for their role in slavery and the slave trade.

The Swanwick Apology was offered some seven months after the May 2007 address of then Jamaican Baptist Union (JBU) President Karl Henlin at the BUGB Assembly in Brighton, where he repeated a call made by the Executive of the JBU for the British Baptist Church to offer an apology for slavery and the slave trade. It may be of interest to note that Henlin, in a report to the JBU, stated as follows: 'That call elicited various kinds of responses and seemed to have struck a nerve, especially among Black Baptists ... it was obvious that the response to the call [would] have serious implications for the ongoing relationships between Black and white Baptists.'

The Swanwick Apology was offered ten years after then JBU General Secretary Trevor Edwards wrote urging British Baptists to make clear and unequivocal statements of 'repentance of the atrocities of chattel slavery, repentance of the acts committed by her foreparents in the name of development and progress; repentance of the acts of exploitation, economic and racial injustice'; he went further to implore British Baptists to 'call upon the State to make restoration of some of the wealth taken from the countries that were former colonies ... this restoration should be made through debt cancellation, aid without strings and cessation of arms sale to repressive dictatorial regimes'.

So, you might better understand why I and several others experienced such a wave of emotions when the apology was finally made. Let me hasten to say, however, that after prayerful consideration, we unreservedly accepted the apology. We were at one with Baptist World Alliance (BWA) General Secretary Neville Callam, who stated, 'We know the joy and the blessing of forgiveness. With this, true healing is possible, and liberation becomes the common gain of everyone involved.'[1]

The question now is: has the apology resulted in an authentic expression of an integrated and non-discriminatory community of believers?

Co-workers but not Co-equals

The JBU and BUGB/BMS story is well documented. We know that it began when George Liele and Moses Baker, early pioneers of Baptist witness in Jamaica, invited the newly formed Baptist Missionary Society (BMS) of London to come and share in their missionary endeavours. By then, Baptist witness was already well established in Jamaica, and hundreds of enslaved people had already accepted the Christian faith.

It is abundantly clear that British Baptists did not come as initiators of the work but in response to a cry for help in organizing the ministry. In spite of this, much to the shame of Jamaican Baptists, it was only in 1983, when we celebrated our bicentenary, that attention began to be given to the pioneering work of Liele. Up to this time, the point of departure for viewing the beginning of Baptist witness in Jamaica was 1814, the arrival of John Rowe, the first missionary from the BMS.

One need not think too hard to discern what may have accounted for this!

Let no one think that I am inviting any devaluation of the collaboration between JBU and British Baptists. On the contrary, I am keenly aware and appreciative of the many blessings God has bestowed on our journey together. In tandem with our British partners, by the end of the nineteenth century Baptist witness was in every parish and many of our pastors were Jamaicans trained at Calabar Theological College; by the middle of the twentieth century, through the Jamaica Baptist Missionary Society (JBMS) and BMS, Jamaican and British

Baptists had spread the good news to other Caribbean islands and Central America.

Education was a significant feature of our collaboration, especially theological, early childhood and secondary, which was emphasized over the years. This focus was evident from very early in the relationship as the Calabar Theological College and Normal School was established in 1843 in Rio Bueno, Trelawny, to train men for ministry and for missionary work in Africa and the Caribbean. Calabar Theological College existed until 1965/1966, when it joined in an ecumenical venture now known as the United Theological College of the West Indies.

Permit me special mention of another product of our working together, namely, the Calabar High School for Boys, which opened its doors on 12 September 1912. It was born out of a pressing need, at the time, to provide sound secondary education for the sons of Baptist ministers. It is a hitherto unchallenged view that Calabar High School has produced more persons in full-time Christian ministry than any other high school in Jamaica. Certainly, within the JBU, no single school has provided more presidents (Devon Dick, Stephen Jennings and Karl Henlin), not to mention a general secretary (Karl Johnson) and many other ministers.

Our cooperation added voice and opposition to the monstrosity of chattel slavery. As Baptists, we were at the forefront of the fight to abolish slavery and to affirm the dignity and development of the African through the establishment of communities of empowerment. While there were those who obeyed the caution from Britain not to involve themselves in 'domestic matters', we celebrate the ones who could not quench the fire of justice that burned within them and played their part in confronting the forces of evil.

The uncomfortable truth, however, is that with all the positives we have recognized, we have to admit that this association did not mean that we were viewed as equals! Understandably the missionaries came as people already culturally conditioned and steeped in the geo-political climate of the day.

Sadly, the church, in its missionary enterprise and even afterwards, played a prominent legitimating and sanctioning role in the status quo established and operated by the imperial and colonial powers. This included not only preaching and teaching aimed at inducing acceptance, by enslaved persons and descendants of enslaved persons, of their status under domination as a religious requirement but also affirming and imposing cultural offerings and social structures that further defined their subject status. The evidence and consequences of this are very well known as an integral part of the history and legacy of colonial and post-colonial societies.

Of course, all of this took place with the supposedly good and sincere intention of evangelizing the pagan peoples. It was, however, at the same time, an exercise that included uncritical collaboration in the expansion and consolidation enterprise of the imperial powers, an evangelizing, civilizing and colonizing mission all in one. This kind of connection of church and imperial power in shared movement and purpose has had a continuing history, even in changing times and in changing forms, but with the same impact.

Whereas the role of the Christian religion seemed ostensibly to have been in service of the imperial and colonial powers as much as anything else, it is not all that can be attributed to it. There were those who had been inspired differently by their religious conviction. They understood their faith commitment from a different perspective. Even though it has not come out as clearly as it ought to have done in many instances, this other perspective originated with the victims of imperialism and colonialism. They saw for themselves that the legitimizing teachings they were receiving, aimed at justifying their condition, did not fit their experience and understanding of God.

Yes, there were and are those who read the Bible differently, and, like Sam Sharpe, Paul Bogle, Martin Luther King Jr, Desmond Tutu and many others, we refuse to be defined as 'less than'.

Are we members one of another? Is this vision a fleeting illusion or faithful pursuit?

Different Times but Same Tune

Is the current landscape any more hopeful of this vision being realized? I would say not, as the same demon or, if you prefer, a phenomenon that has dogged human civilizations and co-opted sections of the church has never died. That is the demon of empire to which we earlier referred as colonialism and imperialism. This phenomenon, marked by a history of rise and fall, decline and succession, is always represented in one form or another, even to the present day.

Given its nature and history, some modern-day representatives of the phenomenon resist or even resent being so styled, with accompanying efforts to disguise that which would identify them as such. Yet there are some intrinsic identifying marks that can never be successfully camouflaged even with the most valiant efforts.

What is empire? Given variations here or there, it may be fairly accurately defined as a political conglomerate constituted of one nation or country exercising dominant control over other territories. This control leaves such territories with no truly effective powers of self-determination in any really significant areas of their existence and operations. Subordination and dependency become their determinative status in the power relations that exist.

While empires may take on different forms and seek to exercise their control in different ways, the status of those under their controlling impact and influence does not change.

The sustaining ideology of empire is one of entitlement, privilege and the assumed right to be in the position in which it is because of its presumed superiority and manifest destiny to be in such a position. Based upon such preconceived assumptions, empires operated on certain principles, disguised and undisguised.

These principles include:

- Conquest and expansionism.
- Domination and subordination.
- Exploitation and oppression.

- Inculturation and ideological indoctrination.
- Social stratification and categorization.
- Reconfiguration and resilience.

Will the missionary enterprise operating from the traditional imperial centres resist or reflect such or some of such principles?

With the rise of neo-nationalism as evidenced in the USA with Trump and here with Brexit, how will British Baptists and the wider church facilitate the realization of this vision: members of one another?

Will our response to the stranger be out of evangelistic pity and piety or fuelled by God's missional mandate to stand alongside a fellow human being?

Interestingly, at this point in time, there has been growing awareness across the board that serious shifts, movements and changes are taking place in the missional dynamics.

Clearly, one of the opportunities that has made itself real is the emergence of fresh possibilities for the missional cause to be pursued as the common cause it was always meant to be, based within a community of integrated, non-discriminatory wholeness. It is a moment for the reappraisal of the essential but varied gifts that are available for the shared commitment, the experience of giving and receiving and of the reciprocity of dependence and interdependence. There is a clear indication of the need for radical overhaul and renewal of relational strategies, respect, acknowledgement and appreciation.

Aren't we seeing, however, that old habits do die hard? The last thing one wants to do amid signs of hope is to emphasize a sense of pessimism that would unnecessarily cast doubt on any real progress that may be in the works. However, the realities themselves are too stubborn to be ignored, and their counter-productive impact too painful to be simply shrugged off. There are some things that demand urgent attention, particularly at traditional originating sources of missional endeavours and also at more recent sources within the same geopolitical spheres.

There are signs that there is an awareness of the new shifts and movements in the missional dynamics. There is a noticeable reconfiguration in the vocabulary of mission and its strategic postures. Yet, for those on the historical underside of the missional enterprise, the reconfigurations are experienced, for the most part, in an odd way that leaves much to be desired.

If truth-speaking in an honest yet loving spirit is in itself cathartic and therapeutic for the speakers and liberating for the hearers, we may take note here of how the reconfigurations are often perceived from the underside.

First, the language of partnership has now come into its own in missional talk, but, in practice, partnership bears distinct signs of patronage. It is placed within the framework and talked about with a self-perception of strength while designating the other as weak, the privileged and the underprivileged, the powerful and the powerless, the independent and the dependent. It is all couched in an ideological definition of those who have and those who are the 'have-nots' having regard to what is considered essential resources.

Another word that has gained much currency but which we hear with suspicion is mutuality. What passes for mutuality is implicitly governed by the consideration given to material superiority, so much so that the real meaning of mutuality is modified. Trust, governance, the value of experience, and knowledge of contextual particularities still tend to be measured and assessed one-sidedly, with the edge given to where material superiority is in evidence. Different ratings are given to resources because they are not valued equally (or even fairly) in partnerships. When Christian partners contribute different resources, those who have the money and the muscle overwhelmingly decide how things are done.

Third, consultations are essentially conducted along the lines of counselling. The process is relegated to a discussion of how predetermined policy conditions are to be met, regulations to be observed and expectations to be met. No one is left in any doubt where such conditionalities are established (become universally applicable). Ideological biases and preconceived stereotypical notions are seen as uppermost; condescension in different forms comes into play to give credence to the consultation label.

Fourth, missional storytelling of shared experiences is really storytelling of benefactors about beneficiaries, rather than of benefactors who are at one and the same time beneficiaries and beneficiaries who are also benefactors.

The greatest danger is that these newly reconfigured approaches may subvert the real opportunity of embracing the missional possibilities as members one of another.

What Sayest Thou, Fleeting Illusion or Faithful Pursuit?

In spite of all the forces that seem to be contending against the realization of this vision, let us affirm that God asks nothing of us that God will not enable us to experience. It is my conviction that we have to continue striving to realize this vision of oneness, dignity, interconnectedness and interdependence.

In so striving, we have to be determined to resist the temptation to assert superiority and the tendency to accept inferiority; we are members one of another!

In so striving, we have to commit to stand in solidarity with each other by opening our eyes to the forces that marginalize and oppose any system that reeks of injustice and dehumanization. If we do not oppose openly, the inference may be that we are supporting silently.

In so striving, we have to be mindful of the battle that we are engaged in. It is a battle for the psyche and souls of persons who have been misused and misled, ostracized and conditioned by centuries of misinformation and lies; it is also a battle for the psyche and souls of those who have been elevated and encouraged to see themselves as superior and entitled.

In so striving, we have to be willing to engage in a number of matters arising, which will involve the following.

Theological/Christian education

It is important to acknowledge that there was a theological construct that legitimized slavery and the slave trade; therefore, it is equally critical that there should be a theological construct and framework that underpin the rooting out of the legacy of slavery. The notion that Blacks were inferior and that the curse of Ham had been placed on us are but two of the lies used historically to keep us in our place; the belief that it was divine providence that Blacks were enslaved so that Africa could be reached with the gospel needs to be debunked.

We cannot be fooled into thinking that all is now well because of the relatively minute numbers of minorities who now occupy places in the corridors of power and privilege. I was intrigued to hear the British Prime Minister referring to some report while stating that racism has no place in this country. Well, if the Prime Minister can openly admit that racism exists, surely the church should have been well aware of it long ago.

Advocacy and activism

If we are members of one another, then we have to be touched by the wrongs done to each other, and on an occasion such as this we cannot blind our eyes or deafen our ears to issues such as reparations and apology. For those who get turned off at hearing these words, especially reparations, let me assure you that as a Black man living in a country that was raped and exploited by representatives of the British Empire, I am not advocating for handouts; as we say in Jamaica, 'I am not begging a money.'

This is an issue of justice. It is undeniable that European wealth, including the capital for the Industrial Revolution, was the direct legacy of the cruel and inhumane system of chattel slavery and the exploitation of slave labour. The landed gentry are still represented in the House of Lords; their opulence is inversely proportional to the economic and social deficit of the African people. Furthermore, the twin evils of racism and the resulting imposed psyche of African self-hate and self-doubt have been skilfully crafted, upheld and fostered over centuries.

The dysfunctional family structure of Africans in the Diaspora in the Caribbean, United Kingdom, Brazil and the USA is a legacy of slavery. The growth in the incidents of violence among people of African descent is the perpetuation of the inculcated self-hate.

A full and unconditional apology is necessary from the heirs and successors of those who perpetrated this monstrous crime and who now enjoy the proceeds and privileges of the wealth accumulated from ill-gotten gain. We do not insist on full and unconditional apology as a condition for the forgiveness of those who were behind the slave trade. If the descendants of formerly enslaved persons had not learnt how to forgive, we would not have survived this long. However, the apology is necessary in order that the forgiveness that is on offer can be appropriated, the healing made complete, and the chapter closed.

This is a minimum requirement. The least that the dignity of the African people deserves is an acknowledgement that this happened, Britain was culpable, and they should hold themselves accountable to contribute in some small way to compensation for the victims of this monstrous crime, their heirs and successors. Compensation is not being sought as a kind of jihad against the sons and daughters of former slave masters. It is necessary, as the fruit of their repentance, to show how completely they have repudiated the monstrosity of slavery and its ill-gotten gain.

If we are members of one another, then you ought to be courageous enough to engage in this conversation within the framework that a wrong has been done and it is full time to do something about it. It is an opportunity to put the legacy of slavery to rest once and for all. This is not in any way to perpetrate the sense of victimhood among African people or to give legitimacy to the caricature of the African who always needs the help of the white man. It is intended to repudiate that legacy and to close that chapter once and for all. Without these actions, chattel slavery and the slave trade that supported it remains an open, festering sore.

In striving for the realization of this vision of the church being and becoming an integrated, non-discriminatory community of believers with a shared commitment to Christ Jesus and empowered by the Spirit to serve a common cause, we have to be open to and dependent upon the Holy Spirit.

It is a journey fraught with pitfalls and challenges; it is a journey that is plagued with frustration and helplessness, and it will not be long before we realize that in our own strength we are doomed to failure. Thankfully God has resourced us with the Holy Spirit, the enabler, sustainer and undergirder.

Let us open ourselves to the Holy Spirit so that we may be on the right side of God as we do what is right in the sight of God.

Let our corporate worship experiences be filled with the move of the Holy Spirit so that we can become a justice movement in the name of Almighty God.

Members one of another? Let's make it our faithful pursuit! And to this end, we pray:

Until the philosophy which holds one race superior and another inferior is finally and permanently discredited and abandoned;
that until there are no longer first-class and second-class citizens of any nation;
that until the color of a man's skin is of no more significance than the color of his eyes;
that until the basic human rights are equally guaranteed to all without regard to race;
that until that day, the dream of lasting peace and world citizenship and the rule of international morality will remain but a fleeting illusion, to be pursued but never attained.
And until the ignoble and unhappy regimes that hold our brothers in Angola, in Mozambique and in South Africa in subhuman bondage have been toppled and destroyed;
until bigotry and prejudice and malicious and inhuman self-interest have been replaced by understanding and tolerance and good-will;
until all Africans stand and speak as free beings, equal in the eyes of all men, as they are in the eyes of Heaven;
until that day, the African continent will not know peace.
We Africans will fight, if necessary, and we know that we shall win, as we are confident in the victory of good over evil.[2]

Notes

1 For the documentation of this instance, see: https://goodfaithmedia.
org/british-baptists-go-to-jamaica-to-apologize-for-slave-trade-cms-
12670/ (accessed 6.6.23).

2 Negusä Nägäst Haile Selassie I, 6 October 1963. Speech to UN,
available at: http://jah-rastafari.com/selassie-words/show-jah-word.asp?
word_id=un (accessed 6.6.23).

6

What Does it Mean to See the Image of God in Each Other?

Revd Bev Thomas, 2016

Sam Sharpe's Biblical Conviction

What does it mean to see the image of God in each other? What I want to do is to explore the historical mindset of the colonies and understand the transformational encounter of Sam Sharpe with God and his word. Let's have a little bit of background about what was going on at the time.

History has a context, a time, a place and a culture, to name but a few; often written from the vantage point of the person who is in charge, the voices of the oppressed are silenced, drowned and sometimes deleted. The voice of Sam Sharpe, and many like him, are voices that will speak to us in the twentieth century with clarity. Just before his death, he is known to have said, 'I would rather die upon yonder gallows than live in slavery.' I'd like to take you back to the mindset of the seventeenth century prior to Sam Sharpe. Sam Sharpe lived in the 1800s; I want to take you back – prior to him.

The English constructed a legal and political structure to govern their labour institution. A man called Thomas Modyford is credited with having bought legal papers from Barbados, one of which was the Act for the Better Ordering and the Governing of Negros. He brought them with him to Jamaica in 1663 when he became the colonist's second governor, and the Jamaican Assembly adopted these papers as their own. The act was to constitute guidelines for New World mastery.

In the passing of laws to govern enslaved individuals, it was the political action of the English to make slavery an English institution. Future generations would inherit the beginning of the narrative of race theory. The language of the law attributed people of African descent with brutishness, an English word associated with beasts. The act came into being citing a history of criminality; slaved persons were insubordinate and head-strong, and past laws were inadequate to control them in any way. Individuals were also described as being heathen, brutish, with an uncertain, dangerous pride of people who required extraordinary punishing laws for the benefit and the good of the colony. Chattel slavery means that one person has total owner-ship of the other. Your personhood was erased in the eyes of the master, and one became property. Within this rule also, there is a distinction between Christian and Negro, and the punish-ment attributed to individuals who were enslaved was based on the fact of whether you were Christian or not. Christian, in this particular perspective, meant white, supporting their belief that individuals were separate and unequal. Because of their views about Africans, men in the assembly could not imagine a person of African descent as legitimately a Christian. Race as a social and ideological construction had not yet emerged, but race as an exercise of power was clearly at work.

Jamaica was the meeting place for very different populations, two of which were the British themselves, in search of quick wealth through sugar, and the Africans – uprooted by force from his or her environment to supply slave labour on which their owner's dream of wealth depended. Samuel Sharpe was born in 1801 into enslavement and brought up in Montego Bay, Jamaica. He was a peer of Mary Seacole, who was born in 1805 in Kingston.

Sharpe learned to read and write and became a deacon in his hometown, in charge of the missionary chapel. Later, the free-dom fighter travelled widely in his parish, preaching about the injustice of slavery, which led to him organizing and leading the general strike in Jamaica. Sharpe kept himself aware of what was going on around him by following the abolition move-ment in Britain, reading newspapers, books and other material.

He must have gone to extraordinary lengths to keep himself informed of what was going on in Jamaica, as the *Jamaican Gleaner*, the national newspaper, was not founded until 1834. The Bible, news and books he read gave him an astute understanding of his times and what he sought to do. He is reported as saying that he relied on the authority of holy Scripture for the view that the white man had no more right to hold the Black man in bondage than the Blacks had to enslave the whites. This was about freedom for all.

On 31 December 1831, Sharpe led the uprising that spread through the whole island and lasted ten days. Over 20,000 of Jamaica's enslaved population were rallied. He was later captured and executed in the market square on 23 May 1832. Shop owners were paid £16 in compensation for their loss of property. Jamaican public theologian Garner Roper said Sharpe, in leading the slave revolt in the British Empire, saved Jamaica from continued bloodshed. The genius of Sharpe is that he rooted the rejection of enslavement and the resistance against slavery in the nature of God. This was the foundation of his rejection and his resistance. His reading imagined a non-violent approach to bring equity. His masters were also his neighbours. This non-violent methodology has been replicated across numerous centuries, nations and religions. The significance of the revolt led by Sharpe has united scholars in agreeing that it accelerated the means that pointed to the end of chattel slavery in the British Empire.

The Mindset of the Twenty-first Century

For clarity, race needs to be distinguished from ethnicity. The latter denotes historic biological heritage. It is not explicitly defined by skin colour, but the association is common in people's minds. In popular thought from the seventeenth century onwards, indigenous roots made you Black in Australia but red in the Western Hemisphere. Roots in Europe defined you as white, roots in Africa as Black; in North and East Asia as yellow, and South Asia as Brown. In a rapidly changing world of people movement, forced and voluntary, are colours helpful in defining people groups as a prefix to thought and colour? Here in Britain, the language of Black and white polarizes and sometimes causes alienation for individuals. Critical thinking can be pushed to the margins because of the prefix 'Black'.

The United Nations Educational, Scientific and Cultural Organization (UNESCO), between 1950 and 1978, issued five statements on the issue of race. This was just after the war. The first on race was called a race question, issued on 18 July 1950; the statement included both a rejection of the scientific basis for theories of racial hierarchies and a moral condemnation of racism. Its first statement suggested, in particular, dropping the term 'race' altogether and speaking instead of ethnic groups, a suggestion that proved to be controversial. In 1978, the General Assembly considered the four previous statements and published a collective declaration on race and racial prejudice, and it stated this:

All human beings belong to a single species ...

All peoples of the world possess equal faculties for attaining the highest level in intellectual, technical, social, economic, cultural and political development ...

The differences between the achievements of the different people groups are entirely attributed to geographical, historical, political, social and cultural factors ...

Any theory which involves the claim that racial or ethnic groups are inherently superior or inferior, thus implying that some would be entitled to dominate and to eliminate others presumed to be inferior, or which bases value judgments on racial differentiation, has no scientific foundation and is contrary to the moral and ethical principles of humanity.[1]

The award-winning poet Claudia Rankine was asked by *The Guardian* recently, 'Why have you written the line in your book?' The interviewer was quoting: 'Because white men can't /

police their imagination / black men are dying.'[2] The response she gave is enlightening:

> When white men are shooting black people, some of it is malice and some an out-of-control image of blackness in their minds. Darren Wilson told the jury that he shot Michael Brown because he looked 'like a demon'. And I don't disbelieve it. Blackness in the white imagination has nothing to do with black people.[3]

Two very different scenarios. The seventeenth century, the twenty-first century. Both of them can engage in a paradigm shift. What allowed Sam Sharpe, in the brutal period that he lived in, to choose to do what he did? He had an engagement with Scripture. And I'd like to read in the light of what you've just heard some verses from Scripture:

> For you created my inmost being;
>   you knit me together in my mother's womb.
> I praise you because I am fearfully and wonderfully made ...
> (Ps. 139.13–14)

> Our Father in heaven,
> hallowed be your name,
> your kingdom come,
> your will be done,
>   on earth as it is in heaven.
> Give us today our daily bread.
> And forgive us our debts,
>   as we also have forgiven our debtors.
> And lead us not into temptation ...
> (Matt. 6.9–13)

> There is neither Jew nor Gentile, neither slave nor free, nor is there male and female, for you are all one in Christ Jesus. (Gal. 3.28)

Do not conform to the pattern of this world, but be transformed by the renewing of your mind. Then you will be able to test and approve what God's will is – his good, pleasing and perfect will. (Rom. 12.2)

The Bible teaches that what gives every human being worth is that we are created in God's image. Who we see in the kingdom of God affects the way that we build the kingdom of God.

In the context of Sam Sharpe, these texts are mind-blowing. They are dangerous and they are freeing. They freed Sam Sharpe's mind. His mind became renewed. He then seeks freedom physically for all. So, his mind has been renewed through the reading of God's word. He is free. What he then goes on to do is seek freedom physically, not just for himself but for all. The essence of racism is prejudice coupled with power. It is rooted in the fallacy that one group of people is superior to another and therefore deserves special privileges based on the colour of their skin, cultural history, ethnic origin or tribal connection. This lie is totally contradictory to the biblical understanding – that all humans are created in the image of God. It all too readily divides people and gives them false permission for oppression and exploitation. Until the dignity of every human being is respected, there needs to be a striving for peace and justice that empowers all members of the human family to live in the fullness of what God intended.

There's a book that I love called *Sisters in the Wilderness*, written by Dolores Williams. A quote from her:

I have come to believe that theologians, in their attempt to talk to and about religious communities, ought to give readers some sense of their autobiographies. This can help an audience discern what helped the theologian to the kind of theology she does. What has been the character of her faith journey? What lessons has this journey taught? What kind of faith inspires her to continue writing and rewriting, living, and reliving in a highly secular white and black world, paying little or no attention to what theologians say?[4]

I have been a trainer now for over 30 years, creating safe spaces for people to talk, to speak and to learn about the historical and current issues surrounding the theme of race, being careful to explain that racism is still with us. In our global living memory, we have witnessed the Ku Klux Klan, who created a living hell for African Americans through their lynching; the Holocaust, where millions of Jews suffered the most appalling suffering, loss of life and degradation; apartheid in South Africa – people in the land of their birth refused the right to vote because of the colour of their skin, tortured in detention without trial and brutal killing; the plight of the Dalits in South Asia, individuals who are forced to live separate lives parallel to mainstream society; and ethnic cleansing in numerous countries. Painful as it is for me to say this: racism also contributed to the narrative of the Brexit vote.

It has now been revealed that hate crimes have gone up 41 per cent since the EU referendum on 23 June 2016. In July 2016, police compared the same month in 2015, and this is according to Home Office figures. I find that absolutely astounding. Assumptions about cultural practices can be very slow to take root. If left unchallenged, they then appear in popular culture and the way languages are used. Consequently, they then become a part of our common law and institutional practices of how we live life as a community. Systematic discrimination and misinformation become the justification for more discrimination. It then creates socially sanctioned attitudes, beliefs, feelings and assumptions, and it generates further misinformation and ignorance. And the cycle goes on.

My experience of training here in the UK – and I have trained mainly in theological colleges for the last 20 years, up and down the country – is that race is still ambiguous, and we're still very nervous talking about it. We are nations uncomfortable in describing our humanity. We use terms like Black and white, and others. Nations and geographical continents describe people groups and heritages in our census and on our official forms. My starting point, both professionally and personally, is encapsulated in this statement: 'The social construct of race does not make the biological existence of race a fact.' The myth of biological race needs to be debunked in our minds and in others. As long as people believe that humanity is naturally divided into biological races, they will give significance and finality to ethnic groups that is not warranted.

Second, there is no conceptual basis for race except for racism. The biblical narrative that liberated Sam Sharpe, a literate and enslaved Baptist preacher who became a freedom fighter, is the same narrative that we read each day. Yet, it does not move us or some of us actively to love our neighbour as we love ourselves. Travelling to Cambridge for many years, I arrived at the train station early in the 2000s, seeing a queue of taxis. I was rather perplexed because usually it is a case that I have to wait for a cab. I jumped into a cab, and the driver complimented me on my English and asked me where I was born. I told him I was born in the Black Country in the West Midlands. He told me that he was also English. I then asked him why there were so many taxis at the taxi rank. It's something that I've never seen before. I opened the floodgate for him to give me an explanation, and I was not prepared for what came out of his mouth. 'These Pakistani men who have come here to take our jobs and to take our houses ...' And I think you know the narrative that went on. And I said nothing for ten minutes as he drove. When I reached the college that I was going to, I asked him if I could have a couple of minutes of his time before I actually paid him, and I made sure I didn't pay him first. I had listened to him for ten minutes, and I think I now needed to speak. In the most humbling way, I said to him this is the same way that my parents were spoken about in the 1950s. When they came to England, they were met with signs: 'No blacks, no Irish, no dogs.' How did he make the assumption that I would not be offended? When did I stop being one of them and become one of us? I don't know when that happened to me. He apologized profusely, and I paid him. I've never seen him since, but I doubt that he'll repeat the narrative in the same way again. Sometimes we forget our story. Those of us who go to church on a regular basis are continually remembering the story and the narrative.

Here in the UK, sometimes we forget. During the Brexit vote, I wasn't in the UK. I decided to take a trip and post my vote. I watched the news and listened to the radio fervently while I was away. The BBC, in their wisdom, decided to interview minority ethnic people here and ask them about how they voted. All of the minority ethnic people that they interviewed voted for Brexit. They had forgotten their narrative. They had forgotten. Here in the UK, we have collective amnesia, sometimes forgetting our own story.

Recently, as in a couple of months ago, I was invited to speak to a group of ministers, which is always an honour. There were about 30 ministers at their bi-monthly meeting. I was invited specifically to speak and address them on racism. I was introduced, I spoke, and during the coffee break one of the ministers came up to me. 'Hello, Miss Thomas,' he said. 'Thank you for coming to speak to us. But nobody told me you were Black.' In my peripheral vision I could see his colleagues disappearing into the wall. None of them came to say anything. I said nothing, and this gentleman went on. 'When I saw you, I asked myself, "Is she trained? Is she competent? Is she qualified? Do I have anything to learn from her?"' Usually, this is something that I know people think, but they don't say. My response to him confused him. My response was, 'Therein lies your challenge. You have to unlearn a whole narrative that you've learned about people like me. Before you should even consider teaching.' And I walked away. During training, I sometimes feel that I have to be who I am not before people choose to hear me. In both of these stories, it causes me to reflect and ask the question, 'Why?' I have learned to be patient towards all that is unsolved in my heart and try to love the questions themselves, like locked rooms, and like books that are not yet written or are written in a foreign tongue. I do not seek the answers that cannot be given to me just now because I may not be able to live them. So, I have learned to live the question. And one day, I might grow into the answer.

Concluding Reflections

Two key questions that hang over my life are: what is commonly understood by the term 'race' here in the UK? The Race Relations Act that we currently have here suggests it is something other than colour, nationality, ethnicity or national origin. So, what is it? Then I want to ask myself the question, has the social construct of race permeated our theology? Does it inform and challenge our preconceptions of 'who is the stranger'? Does it reflect in our ministry? Does it reflect in power and partnership? Does it reflect in the selection of training? What does diversity mean in the context of how we do theology? What does unity mean? And what does equality mean? My ministry over the last 30 years has been growing into those answers.

I asked participants whom I was training to be ministers, 'Who do you see in the kingdom of God?' I hesitate to ask this question any more because of the response I got. An individual responded enthusiastically, 'People like me!' The silence in the room was tangible. I was the only minority ethnic person in the room, and I kept the silence until the participant recognized what he had said. *Who we see in the kingdom of God reflects the way that we build the kingdom of God.*

Sharpe saw himself in the narrative you read and was able to articulate that his current circumstances were not reflecting who he was in God. He wilfully chose not to embrace his paradigm as it was at the time, but he embraced a paradigm shift as a personal and private encounter – and he made it public too. Knowing the cost, he was fully committed to the liberation of others also. So I asked myself the question, why are we still here? Could it be that it is sometimes because we privatize our Christianity?

Chris Boeskool makes a few statements that resonate with me.

'When you're accustomed to privilege, equality feels like oppression.'

'Equality can feel like oppression. But it's not. What you're feeling is just the discomfort of losing a little bit of your privilege.'[5]

There are still sections of our society that are physically present yet socially and economically invisible right here in the UK. Kameron Carter, in his book called *Race: A Theological Account*,[6] urges Black theologians to look back beyond the Enlightenment and the rise of race theory and to bring theology pertaining to the fathers of the church and their writings into conversation with the modern construct of a race and being. I would suggest that all theologians should do this, as it speaks to the heart of how we love our neighbour as we love ourselves.

Take away the noise of your songs;
   I will not listen to the melody of your harps.
But let justice roll down like water,
   and righteousness like an ever-flowing stream.
(Amos 5.23–24)

Of Issachar, those who had understanding of the times, to know what Israel ought to do. (1 Chron. 12.32)

Who are those people among us who have that understanding of the time? And know what should be done? In our global village, there are cries of injustice. There are cries for justice. Who will comfort these individuals? In our global village, cries of justice will confront us with the sin of racism. It is still very much alive. Living and breathing. Around us in all sectors of the literal reality of too many. Who is listening? Do we still live separate and parallel lives?

I want to speak personally to those individuals who have migrated here to the UK and ask the question, 'Who is crying for the current individuals who are migrating here to the UK?' My plea is if this was about us, we would hear voices. I don't believe that we can afford not to say something in the light of the current people movement that is going on here in the UK. We have a responsibility, because we have been there, to say what is going on and to speak. Every time I pray the Lord's Prayer, I pray, 'your kingdom come on earth'. I am reminded of the kingdom of God. Who do you see in the kingdom of God? People from every ethnic group, tribe and nation, worshipping around the throne of God, some people as Black or white, or different races – it is a very narrow perspective on looking at people, and it's a false viewing of how we view humanity. This narrow way or false viewing sometimes feeds our insecurities, judging people and nations by a single narrative. The Bible is the most revolutionary book that I know of. Renewing one's mind is what we should strive for. If allowed to transform our minds, it will transform our community and the earth that we share.

Notes

1 The full 'Declaration on Race and Racial Prejudice' (1978) can be accessed at: https://en.unesco.org/about-us/legal-affairs/declaration-race-and-racial-prejudice (accessed 6.6.23).

2 Rankine, Claudia (2015), *Citizen*, London: Penguin Books.

3 The full interview can be accessed at: www.theguardian.com/books/2015/dec/27/claudia-rankine-poet-citizen-american-lyric-feature (accessed 6.6.23).

4 Williams, Delores S. (1993), *Sisters in the Wilderness: The Challenge of Womanist God-talk*, Maryknoll, NY: Orbis Books.

5 The full blog can be accessed at: www.huffpost.com/entry/when-youre-accustomed-to-privilege_b_9460662 (accessed 6.6.23).

6 Carter, Kameron J. (2008), *Race: A Theological Account*, Oxford: Oxford University Press.

7

Rebellion and Righteousness
– The Foundations of Faith?

Revd Dr Joel Edwards, 2015

Whenever I have the privilege of talking about an iconic figure, my immediate tendency is to paint their achievements on a much wider canvas. My own view is that great heroes are constrained by a reading of their work that freezes them into our own politicized construct. Consequently, a Nat Turner, Paul Bogle or Sam Sharpe, shoe-horned into a Black History Month, may, paradoxically, become smaller as a result. So, I want to discuss Sharpe against the wide lens of Christian religion.

Fallacies about Faith

Religion in general, and Christianity in particular, has been blamed for many atrocities in the world. The absolute claims and intolerance of religious dogma, it is said, are responsible for war and terrorism. But there is also a misleading idea about faith that has grown up with Christian piety. It is the notion that Christian faith is little more than a political pacifier. In the statement attached to Karl Marx, religion is the opiate of the masses. Peace with God, turning the other cheek, peacemaker status and loving your enemy all amount to a comprehensive passivism that neutralizes Christians from political passion.

Historians tell us that during the European revolutions of the nineteenth century, Wesley's revival played a major role in averting revolution in Britain. And it used to be said that the

House of Lords is the Church of England at prayer. The truth is that, to a very large extent, the church has colluded with this idea. It is a failure of the church in the rise of Nazism. But from a Christian perspective, history is a cyclical story of renewal, apostasy, repentance and redemption. This narrative is not concerned with the external trappings of our cultures or traditions: wearing hats or jewellery, going to the cinema or not, smoking or drinking alcohol. And equally, the cycle of renewal has no real interest in our denominations. God is no more a Baptist than he is an Anglican, Methodist or Redeemed Christian Church of God.

Apostasy is the refusal to submit to God's sovereignty and the moral order of justice mandated for human relationships. And this moral order is not limited to 'Christian nations'. The radical claim of the Christian faith is that God rules everywhere and has a moral contract on all human relationships. Whatever else you make of the apocalyptic writings of Daniel and Revelation or the story of Esther in Persia, this is the takeaway message: God is in control.

The cornerstone of this idea is summarized in a timeless statement: "'Love the Lord your God with all your heart and with all your soul and with all your strength and with all your mind"; and, "Love your neighbour as yourself"' (Luke 10.27). The text is striking for a number of reasons. It has its foundations not in the New Testament but in Leviticus (Lev. 19.18, 34). It is then picked up in other New Testament passages (Matt. 22.39; Mark 12.31, 33; Luke 10.27; Rom. 13.9; Gal. 5.14; James 2.8).

Even more than the Ten Commandments, this teaching is described as the summary of all the laws and prophets. So, this is not merely doing good deeds or providing a moral gesture. It is the summary of God's moral law. It is quintessentially God's aspiration for the social order. Every human atrocity, injustice or inequality is judged by this statement. And this is not humanism. Neither is it to be equated to Rousseau's *Social Contract* or Paine's *Rights of Man*. It is fundamentally theological because God interposes himself in the relationship: 'I am the Lord.' It is, so to speak, the equation for a timeless trinity of interpersonal consciousness: God, me, my neighbour.

Consequently, it is the foundation of a New Testament ethic based not only on the idea that all people are created in the image of God but that, ultimately, Jesus as the New Hu/man fulfils the law and reinforces this commandment in the Sermon on the Mount. It means, then, that the moral order of God is indispensable to our social order. So to speak, God has the patent on social order. And this social order is totally fixated on the defence of the 'last' and the 'least of these'. In James' words: 'Religion that God our Father accepts as pure and faultless is this: to look after orphans and widows in their distress and to keep oneself from being polluted by the world' (James 1.27).

The Bible gives us the most succinct and clearest definition of what religion is all about in the combination of these ideas: 'love God, your neighbour and yourself' and take care of widows and orphans – the most vulnerable people on the planet – and do not let the world contaminate you. These ideas provide the main beam of our moral universe and preserve justice in the world.

As an important aside, there is no suggestion here that God is a universalist. There is no contradiction between the universal nature of God's morality and the particularity of his holiness. As William McDowell's song goes, 'You were on your throne, You are God alone.'[1] God's crown of sovereignty is not on auction. But within the framework of God's social order, his justice and morality are non-confessional. It does not belong to Christians alone. The moral law, inherent in the image of God, belongs *to* everyone and demands accountability *from* everyone. It has nothing to do with religious creed. The breadth of God's moral law is best summed up in the anti-clerical story of the good Samaritan (Luke 10).

In the 'love-God-your-neighbour-and-yourself' equation, the fear of God takes away fear of 'the other'. It is a formulation that is meant to drive our moral universe, our spirituality, domestic relations, economic and foreign policy, education, health and immigration.

Religion and Righteousness

The role of Christian religion is, therefore, to resist anything that militates against this divine moral order. As Paul puts it, 'We demolish arguments and every pretension that sets itself up against the knowledge of God, and we take captive every thought to make it obedient to Christ' (2 Cor. 10.5).

Christian faith offers a *bespoke righteousness* that rebels against a status quo of apostasy – that is, mindsets, spiritualities and systems that work against the world as God intends it to be. Christian faith is rebellion against the status quo of unrighteousness – and as someone once said, the status quo is Latin for the mess we are in!

Our problem with 'righteousness' is that we have placed rather narrow parameters around it. But biblical righteousness is expansive. In the wisdom of Proverbs, 'Righteousness exalts a nation, but sin condemns any people' (Prov. 14.34). It is a well-known text with unexplored application. But a righteousness that lifts a nation must have the force of a moral eco-system, preserving well-being and wholeness for all its citizens. The righteousness of religion should have private and public benefit.

The Bible's belief in justice is crucial for our understanding of a transformed world. 'Justice' (*dikaiosune*) is the catalysing arrangement that bridges the gap between our relationship with God and our material relationship with those around us. The New Testament Greek Lexicon defines 'justice' as 'the doctrine concerning the way in which man may attain a state approved by God'. But it also describes it as 'integrity, virtue, purity of life'. Here, anthropology meets theology. The biblical evidence is that there is no theological or moral distinction between the ideas of holiness, righteousness and justice. It is an educational study to go through the Scriptures and identify those passages of the Bible in which all three ideas are held together. Perhaps one of the best examples is found in Isaiah: 'But the LORD Almighty will be exalted by his *justice*, and the *holy* God will show himself holy by his *righteousness*' (Isa. 5.16). Holiness, righteousness and justice form a trinity of interpersonal virtues by which the holiness 'accounted' to us exclusively through faith in Jesus expresses itself communally in Christian neigh-bourliness and becomes translated in our biblical response to institutional or systemic evil. In Wesley's terms, 'The gospel of Christ knows of no religion, but social; no holiness but social holiness.'[2]

Righteousness calls for rebellion against every value or vehicle that fails to comply with the world as God meant it to be. This is explicit in the radical behaviour of the Old Testament prophets who opposed injustice, extortion and land-grabbing. It is amplified in Jesus' behaviour in the Temple, John the Baptist who challenged Herod, and the apostles who said they would rather obey God than man.

Religion that colludes with oppression is, therefore, an irrele-vant imposter of righteousness. Unrighteous religion fails to look out for the orphans and the widows because it has already become polluted by the world. This polluted faith fails to under-stand the rebellion against the godless worship condemned in Isaiah, Amos and Micah. 'He has shown you, O man, what is good. And what does the LORD require of you? To act justly, and to love mercy and walk humbly with your God' (Mic. 6.8). Where faith fails to rebel, it fails its foundation and is out of alignment with its Chief Cornerstone.

Religion and Realignment

This has been the nature of Christian apostasy for the past 2,000 years. Church history is essentially a catalogue of rebel-lions seeking realignment to God and neighbour. Church history is not simply a struggle for a return to pure doctrine. It has also been a struggle for revolutionary behaviour in line with God's moral order. It is worth remembering that the very first Christian controversy was not about doctrine but about the racist treatment of Greek widows in the extended com-munity (Acts 6.1–7). This rebellion has been a combination of internal Christian conflicts, of which Luther's Ninety-Five Theses and the Reformation was a crucial example. William Tyndale, who gave us our first English translation of the Bible, has been described as God's Outlaw. Cromwell, the Puritans and the Pilgrim Fathers have all been imperfect contributors in the battle for a bespoke righteousness that upholds the rule of law, religious freedom and human rights.

But the Christian rebellion has also risen up in civil disobedience to rage against the night of injustice and 'man's inhumanity to man'. Collectively we have rebelled against the tortures of the Middle Passage, child factory labour and chimney sweeps and South African apartheid. So American civil rights and Black people who refused to give up their seats on the buses, Catholic bishops against Latin American dictators and drug lords, and American missionaries resisting the Shining Path in Peru have all been a part of the rebellion of our bespoke righteousness.

Most heroes have not been celebrated. The irrepressible nature of the human spirit and the power of the Spirit have joined forces in a thousand silent rebellions against the enemies of God's social order. The girl who stood up to the bully and 'The Entertainer' shops firmly shut on a Sunday have all been a part of a religious No! to the pollution of the world. In Brueggemann's words, 'We are not summoned to be an echo of culture, either to administer its economics, to embrace its psychology or to certify its morality. To us is gifted an alternative way.'

> Those who hope in Christ can no longer put up with reality as it is, but begin to suffer under it, to contradict it. Peace with God means conflict with the world, for the goad of the promised future stabs inexorably into the flesh of every unfulfilled present.[3]

Sam Sharpe and Rebellious Righteousness

And this brings us to Sam Sharpe. As a literate and influential Baptist deacon, Sharpe was already known as a leader who had a close relationship with his missionary pastor, Revd Thomas Burchill. Devon Dick suggests that at the time of his rebellion and execution, 23 May 1832, Sharpe was between 25 and 26.[4] However, popular opinion is that Sharpe was born in 1800.

It is hard to know if, in his own eyes, Sam Sharpe set out to do anything spectacular on 27 December 1831. But he was certainly purposeful. Sharpe's passive resistance was an early and bold example of a calculated industrial action. The strike action was to insist that following their three-day Christmas holidays, slaves should be paid for their work. If their request was refused, the slaves were to withdraw labour precisely at the time when the cane was ready to harvest. This was an economic calculation: payment over against wasted crop.

The plan went horribly wrong, and after the initial burning of the crops at the Kensington Estate, actions escalated into a full-scale rebellion that lasted ten days, leaving over 500 slaves and ten whites killed. As Sharpe resigned himself to the gallows, he declared that he would rather be hung than remain a slave. Two things catalysed Sharpe's rebellion. The first was his understanding of the Bible. But this was a reading of the Bible that flowed within the nonconformist tradition of the Baptist movement. My point here is that Sharpe's behaviour was not just the courage of a Black brother in revolt! Sharpe's reaction is to be understood in the continuum of the rebellion for a bespoke righteousness. He was not an isolated Black vigilante. His biblical paradigm was this: no one can serve two masters.[5] It followed, therefore, that, theologically, slavery as an industrial and economic construct was bankrupt, and he wanted to change it by passive resistance.

Second, Sharpe based his actions on political analysis. His ability to read meant that he was acutely aware of the abolitionist movement, fuelled in part by Baptist sentiments. But he was also aware of the extensive parliamentary debates taking place in the House of Commons. The general consensus is that Sharpe mistakenly thought that abolition was either imminent or had already taken place and that his industrial action would in some way be vindicated by parliamentary actions.

As we now know, slavery was abolished in 1834. But Sharpe's protest took place in the political aftermath of the Abolition of the Slave Trade in 1807 and the founding of the Anti-Slavery Society in 1823. The ferment of abolitionism was a part of Sharpe's political environment. As Dr Muir reminds us, after

1808 the influx of Black slaves to the Caribbean and America was negligent and, 'The world in which Sam Sharpe conducted his rebellion was a world in moral and economic transition. It was a world of revolutionary possibilities.'[6]

To return to his political context, Sharpe stood in the revolutionary slipstream of the incredible revolution in 1800 in Haiti, where the ex-slave Toussaint Louverture resisted Napoleon and established the first nation of former slaves. He would have been very aware of the new Negro colony of Free Town in Sierra Leone established in 1787–92.

In the USA, at least three rebellions would have been common knowledge: on 7 October 1800, General Gabriel, 'the Black Samson', was executed for insurrection; in 1822, the Methodist Denmark Vesey's ambitious plot in North Carolina was stymied; and on 11 November 1831 – just a few days before Sharpe's rebellion – Nat Turner was hanged for his plot against Virginia slave owners. What may have influenced Sharpe's non-violence was that in each case, the US rebellions, though directly influenced by their reading of the Bible, were all committed to the wholesale slaughter of plantation owners. As Wilmore reminds us,

Nat Turner, like others whose names are buried under the debris of the citadel of American slavery, discovered that the God of the Bible demanded justice, and to know him and his Son Jesus Christ was to be set free from every power that dehumanizes and oppresses.[7]

But even more significantly, the literate Sharpe would have been aware that the rebellious zeitgeist of the period in which he was born was not confined to Black rebellion. The battlefields of Europe were testaments to the thirst for freedom: Waterloo in 1815, and battles for independence raged throughout 1830 in the Netherlands, Switzerland, Poland, Italy and Belgium.

If Sharpe did misread the political signals in the British parliament, he could have been forgiven for doing so. For it is likely that his political calculations were influenced by an enormous groundswell for abolition sustained over a 30-year period. On

15 May 1830, an abolitionist meeting at Exeter Hall presented an unprecedented 172,000 signatures for abolition to the UK parliament.[8]

Sharpe's rebellion was a crucial chapter in the cyclical rebellion for authentic faith, and the moral order and his behaviour cannot be fully appreciated apart from the environment of rebellion in which his own political surveillance took place.

And of even more significance, Sam Sharpe's actions may well have drawn inspiration from the missionary movement that galvanized abolition during his lifetime. Quakers, now established champions of abolition, expelled all slave owners in 1774 and released all their slaves in 1776. It is inconceivable that Sharpe would not have heard of the Demerara emancipation movement of the Baptist missionary John Smith between 1817 and 1824.

In 1809 the Church Missionary Society (CMS) was proposing to send Black people from the West Indies and the US as missionaries to Africa.[9] In 1830, the Black Baptist Richard Pinnock was baptized with his eldest daughter and took the Lord's Supper from the Baptist missionary John Clarke.[10] And when in 1830, a Black Baptist, Sam Swiney, was found guilty of preaching without his master's consent, yet another abolitionist Baptist missionary, William Knibb, took up his case.[11]

Devon Dick's *Rebellion to Riot*, outlining the Jamaican church's contribution to nation-building during and after slavery, identifies Baptist ambivalence to Sharpe's rebellion.[12] But even so, the powerful lobby of missionaries was a compatible theological sound-check for his radical voice. At a London meeting in 1832, William Knibb estimated that there were over 20,000 Baptists in Jamaica.[13]

And this was significant because the engine for abolition was moving away from a few established voices of the Wilberforce kind to the impatient nonconformist movements. In 1823, parliament received six Anglican petitions and one nonconformist petition. In 1826, five Anglican petitions against six nonconformists. In 1830, there were three Anglican petitions compared to 70 nonconformists.[14] This meant that the more coercive role of conversion envisaged by the established plantation owners[15] was being replaced by the abolitionist theology of the noncon-formists. As David Brian Davis claims, 'The main thrust of eighteenth-century revivalism ended with the missionary not the abolitionist.'[16]

If we are to benefit from Sharpe's participation in bespoke righteousness, we should learn the power of this twofold per-spective that motivated him to act with such imagination and courage.

A biblicism that ignores political realities is likely to neutralize God's rebellion against unrighteousness. It makes us the pious pawns of our political leaders who are happy to attend our conventions and public gatherings to be applauded and prayed for without being held accountable for political righteousness.

So many of our churches attract public figures as a matter of course – something we should be commended for. But there is now scope for a rebellious reading of the Scriptures, which makes us more prophetic in the counter. In this reading, we must go beyond narrating the anti-clerical story of the good Samaritan in terms of good social work, for as Martin Luther King suggests,

> We are called to play the Good Samaritan on life's roadside, but that will be only an initial act; true compassion is more than flinging a coin to a beggar. It comes to see that an edifice which produces beggars needs restructuring.[17]

Good leadership, says Archbishop Rowan Williams, is the church 'obstinately asking the State about its accountability and the justification of its priorities',[18] and helping people to ask the right questions.[19] When we fail to do so, we are in danger of worshipping while being passive co-conspirators with unright-eousness. But biblical rebellion also works with the grain of political and economic realities. Like Moses in Egypt and Esther in Persia, rebellion works with political intelligence in order to prevent oppression from degenerating into total oblivion. And yet our reading of political realities is never done in isolation from our biblical framework. To leave the Bible behind is to make us political activists alone. This was the substantial difference between King and the Black Power Movement. Our calling is wider and far more enduring. Our righteous rebellion as a foundation of Christian faith will always and inevitably bring us into collaboration with non-Christian co-workers for rightness. But our calling is to bring our church to realignment with the mission of God. Our mission in the world is to call society to stand behind the yellow line where it is safer for everyone. Ultimately it is to love God, your neighbour and yourself.

I believe that this is the legacy of Sam Sharpe, the Baptist deacon and rebel for righteousness.

Notes

1 McDowell, William (2011), 'You are God Alone', on *Arise*, Los Angeles: Entertainment One.

2 Wesley, John (1739), 'Preface', *Hymns and Sacred Poems*.

3 Moltmann, Jürgen (2010), trans. James W. Leitch, *Theology of Hope*, London: SCM Press.

4 Dick, Devon (2012), 'Lessons from Sam Sharpe', *The Gleaner*, 24 May. Dick suggests in his 2009 book *The Cross and Machete: Native Baptists of Jamaica*, Kingston: Ian Randle Publishers, that his own research disputes this.

5 Matthew 6.24; Luke 16.13.

6 Muir, R. David (2014), *Slavery, Abolition and Diasporan Memory and the Curious Invisibility of Sam Sharpe from Baptist Centenary Historiography*, a discussion paper, October, Oxford: Regent's Park College.

7 Wilmore, Gayraud S. (1986), *Black Religion and Black Radicalism: An Interpretation of the Religious History of Afro-American People*, Maryknoll, NY: Orbis Books, p. 64.

8 Jakobsson, Stiv (1972), *Am I Not a Man and a Brother? British Missions and the Abolition of the Slave Trade and Slavery in West Africa and the West Indies 1786–1838*, Uppsala: Gleerup, p. 448.

9 Extract, Butschar to Nyländer, 16 September 1809, from Klein to Pratt, 21 July, in Proceedings of CMS, 1812.

10 Clarke, John (1850), 'Memoire of the Late Rev. Joseph Merrick', *The Baptist Magazine* 5.8, April, pp. 197–204. Available at: https://biblicalstudies.gospelstudies.org.uk/articles_baptist-magazine_03.php (accessed 30.6.23).

11 *Anti-Slavery Monthly Reporter*, vol. IV, no. 77, 1 March 1831.

12 Dick, Devon (2002), *Rebellion to Riot: The Jamaican Church in Nation Building*, Kingston: Ian Randle Publishers, p. 68.

13 Jakobsson, *Am I Not a Man and a Brother?*, p. 480.

14 Drescher, Seymour (1982), *Capitalism and Anti-Slavery*, New York: Macmillan Press.

15 See Bennett Jr, J. Henry (1958), *Bondsmen and Bishops: Slavery and Apprenticeship on Codrington Plantations in Barbados, 1710–1838*, Los Angeles, CA: University of California Press.

16 Davis, David Brian (1970), *The Problem of Slavery in Western Culture*, New York: Cornell University Press, p. 388.

17 King Jr, Martin Luther (1967), 'A Time to Break Silence', speech at Riverside Church, New York.

18 Williams, Rowan, 'European Faith and Culture', lecture at the Anglican Cathedral in Liverpool, Europe's Capital of Culture 2008, and in Spencer, Nick (2006), *Doing God*, London: Theos.

19 Christian Aid AGM, 15 October 2013.

8

Deconstructing the Notion of Race

Revd Dr Neville Callam, 2013

[F]rom the hour of their birth, some men are marked out for subjection, others for rule ... It is clear that just as some are by nature free, so others are by nature slaves, and for these latter the condition of slavery is both beneficial and just. (Aristotle)[1]

Greeks were born to rule barbarians, Mother, not barbarians to rule Greeks. They are slaves by nature; we have freedom in our blood. (Euripides)[2]

The Black skin is not a badge of shame, but rather a glorious symbol of ... greatness. (Marcus Mosiah Garvey)[3]

The absolute equality of races, physical, political and social is the founding stone of the world and human achievement ... [T]he voice of Science, Religion, and practical Politics is one in denying the God-appointed existence of super-races or of races naturally and inevitably and eternally inferior. (Pan-African Congress, 1921)[4]

[T]he social construction of race does not make the biological existence of race a fact. The myth of biological race needs to be debunked in our minds and in others'. As long as people believe that humanity is 'naturally' divided into biological races, they will give a significance and finality to ethnic groups that are not warranted. (Eloise Meneses)[5]

There is no conceptual basis for race except racism. (Charles Hirschman)[6]

Introduction

There are four main reasons why this evening's assignment gives me much pleasure.

The first is the opportunity it affords me to visit the United Kingdom once again. It has never ceased to amaze me that, at the height of its power, this small country maintained control over such a vast portion of the earth! By 1914, apart from its own population of 46 million, Britain ruled 400 million people around the world,[7] and by 1922, Britain controlled the world's largest empire with a population of 458 million, comprising one-fifth of the existing world population and covering nearly 25 per cent of the world's land space.[8]

It is also amazing how the perception of this country has changed over the years. Consider this: the Greek orator Cicero once gave what he no doubt considered wise counsel to his friend, Atticus. This is what he said: 'Do not obtain your slaves from Britain because they are so stupid and so utterly incapable of being taught that they are not fit to form a part of the household of Athens.'[9]

Later, in the seventh century, a North African, one of the Moors who had conquered Spain, described Northern Europeans in the following way: 'They are of cold temperament and never reach maturity. They are of great stature and of a white colour. But they lack all sharpness of wit and penetration of intellect.'[10] How things have changed! Today, hardly anyone would paint a portrait of the people of this country in those unflattering terms. Nor could anyone justifiably do so now and perhaps also ever!

The second reason for my pleasure at this appointment is the opportunity to be here in the British Midlands, where my father, who was among those who came to England in the wave of migration from the Caribbean after the Second World War,[11] spent 13 years of his adult life contributing to the development of this great country. He came to the UK in order to ensure that he could fulfil his economic responsibility as a husband and father. As soon as his two youngest children were close to completing their secondary education in their home country, he returned to Jamaica and shared with the family stories of his experience overseas. None of the children my father returned to embrace in Jamaica considered migration to the United Kingdom an option to be pursued, but they were grateful for what this country helped their father to do.

The third reason for the pleasure I find in addressing you today is the opportunity this lecture affords me to be associated with the Sam Sharpe Lecture series. I am particularly grateful that the committee responsible for these lectures accepted my proposal of the subject of race as the focus for this lecture. Especially when we remember the one whose life and contribution inspired this lecture series, it is entirely appropriate that we should consider the subject of race, laying bare the vastness and the pernicious nature of the sin reflected in an understanding of race as a biological reality. Our goal is to clearly identify what lies at the core of the insidious understanding of race as a property of human beings rather than a socially constructed identity and to expose some of its dangerous implications.

In Birmingham

Fourth, I gratefully acknowledge the opportunity to deliver this Sam Sharpe Lecture here in this city of Birmingham. In my preparation for today, I recalled the way English slave trader William Snelgrave characterized the opinion of British slave traders during the eighteenth century:

> Tho' to traffic in human creatures may at first sight appear barbarous, inhuman and unnatural, yet the traders herein have as much to plead in their own excuse as can be said for some other branches of trade, namely, the *advantage* of it ... In a word, from this trade proceeds benefits far outweighing all either real or pretended mishaps and inconveniences.[12]

Yesterday, I was in Manchester, which was the centre of the cotton trade during the nineteenth century. Here in Birmingham, I have come to what was once the centre of the gun trade. Let noted Caribbean historian Eric Williams explain:

Slave trading demanded goods more gruesome than woollen and cotton manufactures; fetters and chains and padlocks were needed to fasten the Negroes more securely on the slave ships ... Iron bars were the trading medium on a large part of the African coast and were equivalent to four copper bars ... Guns formed a regular part of every African cargo. Birmingham was the centre of the gun trade.[13]

In the eighteenth century, Birmingham supplied the sugar stoves, rollers for crushing cane, wrought iron and nails needed on the plantations in the West Indies. In Africa, Birmingham guns were exchanged for men and, as Eric Williams states, 'it was a common saying that the price of a Negro was one Birmingham gun'.[14] In the late eighteenth century, Birmingham admitted its manufacturing industry's considerable dependency on the slave trade. Birmingham's businessmen explained that 'Abolition would ruin the town and impoverish its inhabitants.'[15] In the nineteenth century, Birmingham guns were exchanged for African palm oil.

Although, right here in Birmingham, a society to abolish slavery was started in 1788 – and we applaud that development – we should not forget the extent to which this city was built on the oppression of Africans in Africa and the exploitation of enslaved Africans in the Caribbean.

Understanding how the United Kingdom flourished as a result of slavery and the slave trade, one of your own citizens, James Boswell (1740–95), once declared:

To abolish a status which in all ages God has sanctioned and man has continued would not only be robbery to an innumerable class of our fellow-subjects, but it would be extreme cruelty to the African savages, a portion of whom it saves from massacre or intolerable bondage in their own country and introduces into a much happier state of life ... To abolish that trade would be to 'shut the gates of mercy on mankind'.[16]

Boswell's claims should surprise no one, for he considered the enslaved state to be superior to life in freedom in Africa. Do you recall what he said in one of his unforgettable poems depicting how happy and fortunate enslaved persons were?

> The cheerful gang! – the negroes see
> Perform the task of industry:
> Ev'n at their labour hear them sing,
> While time flies quick on downy wing;
> Finish'd the bus'ness of the day,
> No human beings are more gay:
> Of food, clothes, cleanly lodging sure,
> Each has his property secure;
> Their wives and children protected,
> In sickness they are not neglected;
> And when old age brings a release,
> Their grateful days they end in peace.[17]

If Boswell's assumptions about race reflected where England was in the eighteenth century, he was not as forthright in his disdainful opinion as was the British Foreign Office in the twentieth century. The manoeuvres of the United States, Britain and Australia resulted in the failure of the 1919 Paris Peace Conference to agree a reasonable proposal for the international community to affirm 'the principle of equality of nations and just treatment of their nationals'.[18] In response, this is what the British Foreign Office stated in a confidential memorandum:

> The 'RACE EQUALITY' question is a highly combustible one … The white and the coloured races cannot and will not amalgamate. One or the other must be the ruling caste … There is, therefore, at present in practical politics no solution to the race question.[19]

I have been encouraged by news of some of the initiatives being taken by churches and their leaders here in the United Kingdom in recent decades to deal with the legacy and the prevalence of the sin of racial prejudice that was once manifested in the enslavement of Black people in the West Indies. Gratefully, the number of forgetful beneficiaries of this legacy seems to be on the decrease.

Churches in countries whose history is marked by the experience of systematically oppressing others through slavery need to ensure that their acknowledgement of the economic benefits they and their communities have reaped from slavery is accompanied by determined efforts to root out racism from within their ranks. They are also called to bear prophetic witness to the wider society on behalf of those who suffer from negative racial profiling. I have come to the conclusion that unless these initiatives include a determined effort to deconstruct the notion of race, the efforts may fairly be characterized as equivalent to polishing dirty floors that were not first scrubbed to remove the unwanted and unsightly particles that stuck to them.

In this lecture, I propose to briefly characterize the relation of ethnicity and human dignity in the thinking of Sam Sharpe, who was one of the collaborators in the project to secure liberation from enslavement for people residing in the Caribbean. After this, I will discuss the emergence and exposure of the myth informing the ideology of race, and then propose certain priority steps that need to be taken if the deconstruction of the idea of race is taken seriously in the ecclesial community.

Sharpe, Human Dignity and Ethnicity

The Right Excellent Samuel Sharpe, National Hero of Jamaica, was born in Jamaica to African parents who had been captured and transported to Jamaica, where they were enslaved.[20] His parents were among the millions of persons of African origin who were forcibly removed from Africa with the intention of enslavement in the Caribbean, North America and South America.[21] Indeed, the transatlantic trade in Africans has been described as

> the largest forced human migration in recorded history. The extent of the human suffering associated with this involuntary relocation of men, women and children may never be known. But their shipment – packed and stored beneath the deck of ships like commodities – constitutes one of the greatest horrors of modern times.[22]

Sharpe accepted the gospel of Jesus Christ preached by formerly enslaved Africans who went to Jamaica with the message of the gospel. His faith was also informed by the teaching of the missionaries sent from among the same European people who undertook to deprive him of his dignity and exploit his labour for pecuniary gain. From his reading of the Bible, Sharpe came to see the fundamental error on which the sin of racism rests – the error that nourished the very roots of the system of slavery as it was practised in the Caribbean. This is the odious belief that Sharpe, and those whose skin colour looked like his, were not to be regarded as people who shared the same dignity and worth as those who exploited them.

Sam Sharpe realized that the oppressive slaveholders believed that he, and others like him, lacked a rightful claim to the humanity the enslavers reserved for themselves. Resolute in his rejection of this belief, Sharpe was willing to offer up his life if his dignity were going to be continually disrespected and his humanity perpetually denied. 'I would rather die on yonder gallows than live in slavery' were the immortal words he declared before his life was taken from him.[23]

Currently, we do not have access to any literary works by Sam Sharpe – the text of sermons he preached and the Bible studies he delivered, for example. On account of this, we are forced to rely on secondary sources for an understanding of what Sharpe believed. Most of the available sources were compiled by members of the oppressor class that sought to deprive Sharpe of his human dignity. Even when statements are attributed to Sharpe, these are reported by Europeans domiciled in Jamaica in the nineteenth century. The cumulative evidence from the available sources suggests the following generalized wording of four of Sharpe's convictions expressed in the language of the contemporary age.

First, all human beings are made by God, who invests in them dignity and rights that are inalienable and inviolable, including the right to be free.

Second, slavery is inconsistent with biblical teaching on human freedom because it fundamentally represents a disregard for the freedom of God and readiness to dehumanize persons.

It is predicated on the idea that enslavers are entitled to exploit the enslaved for their own material advantage. Sharpe's belief that slavery represents the commodification of the enslaved and their exploitation for the benefit of the enslavers is what lay at the very foundation of the Baptist War. Asked about the origin of his idea that all people have a right to be free, Sharpe identified the Bible as the source from which he gained the idea.[24]

Third, since slavery represents a denial of human dignity, the enslaved have an obligation to take non-violent action to secure their freedom. If in the pursuit of their liberty through non-violent protest, they encounter violence from those who oppress them, the enslaved are entitled to act in self-defence.

Fourth, it seems reasonable to assert that Sharpe understood that considerations of ethnicity were fundamental to the operation of the plantation economy in which Black people were forced to serve the interests of white people. There is no avoiding the question of ethnicity and 'race' when we are reflecting on the legacy of the honourable Samuel Sharpe.

Sharpe knew that the practice of slavery in the Caribbean was undergirded by racist presumptions. According to Methodist missionary Henry Bleby, Sharpe witnessed to having 'learnt from his Bible that the whites had no more right to hold black people in slavery than the black people had to make the white people slaves; and for his own part, he would rather die than live in slavery'.[25] Sharpe did not believe white people had any right to make merchandise of a human being. For him, slavery was 'a monstrous injustice'.[26]

Like Sharpe, many of the Africans who suffered the scourge of slavery felt the brunt of the violent disrespect for their dignity and humanity. They resisted the determined resolve of the estates to extract and benefit from their labour without adequately compensating them. Eventually, many turned to violent protest as a last resort.

When Sharpe's forebears passed through the door of no return,[27] the captured Africans did not know what awaited them in the so-called New World. However, they would have had a premonition of it when piled up in a cellar like the one at the place now called the Slave Castle in Ghana; they suffered brutal dehumanization while hearing the joyful sounds of Anglicans at worship in the room under which they were incarcerated.[28]

Arriving in the Caribbean and sold to European business-men by European traders, the enslaved lost every semblance of self-determination. They were now listed as part of the merchandise on the sugar estate on which they were forced to work.[29] Enslaved people in western Jamaica responded to the denial of their humanity, the violation of their dignity and the exploitation of their labour. They decided that beginning immediately after Christmas 1831, they would cease working until those who robbed them of the benefits of their toil were ready to offer them meaningful compensation. All they were expecting was 2s 6p per week, the amount paid to so-called 'workhouse men'.[30]

What Sharpe really desired was the purchase of freedom through the medium of a massive work stoppage. What eventuated, however, was the dusty brilliance of the night-time sky as the enslaved put sugar cane plantations and buildings to the torch on the evening of 27 December 1831.[31] To use the words of Methodist missionary Henry Bleby, 'It was not Sharpe's purpose to wade through blood to freedom, although he himself was prepared to die in pursuit of freedom.'[32] Yet, it was for that work stoppage and its subsequent rampage that he and several hundred others were executed. Today, close to 200 years later, I am presenting a lecture in Sharpe's honour here in the land that produced the rascals who exploited Sharpe's labour in slavery and then deprived him of his life. Delroy Reid-Salmon[33] claimed that, after 'excavating the layers of ... mythology that engulf ... the human subject in history',[34] he had mined the thought that Sharpe affirmed the equality of all human beings and the divine gift of freedom for everyone. Reid-Salmon offers a compelling interpretation of Sharpe's theological anthropology.

The Emergence and Exposure of the Myth Undergirding Race Ideology

Slavery existed long before the Europeans built a monument in its honour in the West Indies, and it assumed many forms over the years.[35] After the Romans abandoned this island (the United Kingdom), which was a remote outpost of their empire, and the Germanic tribes captured it, some of the people who lived here were sold into slavery.

It was the 'civilized' Romans who introduced slavery to the 'barbarians' of Western Europe, to borrow the description of Jamaican historian Richard Hart, who is familiar with the terms employed by the slavers of those days.[36] It is said that, at the start of the eleventh century, nearly 10 per cent of the British population was enslaved.

After Muslims from North Africa conquered the Iberian Peninsula from the Romans, they repelled their attackers and enslaved those whom they took as prisoners of war. Over much of their period of dominance, between 711 and 1492, the Muslims in Iberia enslaved both Blacks and whites. As James Sweet has shown,[37] they introduced 'invidious distinctions' between Black and white slaves, naming them differently – *abd* and *mamluk* – and treating them differently. White slaves served mainly as household helpers, and Blacks were assigned the arduous tasks that needed to be done. Even free Blacks were identified as *abid* (plural of *abd*).[38]

White Iberians living in the context of the prevailing Muslim attitude to Blacks shared that attitude themselves. And when the days of Iberian subjugation by the Moors came to an end, the Spanish and Portuguese powers, during the fourteenth century, looked for a zone over which to exert control and to expand their sphere of influence. They turned their attention to the south and west. By this time, however, they had already espoused notions of the inferiority of Blacks which, in the eighteenth century, were refined by Europeans, presenting themselves as scientists, into an identifiable and clear racist ideology that predicated Black inferiority on biological criteria.

What resulted from the Iberian expansion project was a form of slavery that reflected the deepest depravity of the human mind. As Hart has said, 'The ancient institution of slavery ... was transplanted to the Americas where it was adapted, almost beyond recognition of its earlier forms, to serve a new commercial purpose. Its horrors were intensified a thousandfold.'[39]

Orlando Patterson's identification of slavery as 'social death' describes very well the form of slavery in the West Indies. The enslaved suffered a 'perpetual state of dishonour',[40] being permanently and violently alienated from others, becoming socially dead.

The point being made is that when Europeans introduced the institution of slavery in the Caribbean, it was in the context of a developing prejudice towards Black people. Slaveholders in the Caribbean were undoubtedly aware that those from whose dehumanization they profited were people whose ethnic origins were different from theirs. It is generally agreed, however, that when the British trade in slaves was at its height, racist thinking had not yet achieved its most heinous form. Over the centuries, the developing ideology of race was to acquire the mask of scientific foundation, which was effective in its power to deceive its subscribers. Scientific racism mischaracterized the notion of race as a biological reality and bequeathed a legacy of white racism that many still struggle to overcome today.

Nor were the Iberians the only ones who helped construct the myth of Blacks as inferior to whites. Other Europeans shared liberally in the manufacture of this most shameful ideological edifice that housed such persons as a bookkeeper from the New Yarmouth plantation in Vere, Jamaica, who, in 1823, informed the governor of Jamaica:

There are a race of beings that cannot bear prosperity ... It will be a lapse of ages before the Negro can even participate of the blessings of freedom; the very name of the African must cease to exist in their memories before their customs are obliterated.[41]

Strengthening the Foundations of Scientific Racism

Many were the Europeans who laid the foundations for the rampant disrespect for human dignity that lies at the very heart of the idea of race. Ivan Hannaford has claimed that 'there is very little evidence of a conscious idea of race until after the Reformation'.[42] Whether this is so or not, as James Sweet has said, 'the treatment of black Africans from the Middle Ages to the early modern period appears to be racism without race'.[43] This is in keeping with Orlando Patterson's observation that 'the absence of an articulated doctrine of racial superiority does not necessarily imply behavioural tolerance in the relations between peoples of somatically different groups'.[44]

The list of people who helped build the edifice of scientific racism is long, and some of the names included in it are likely to surprise those who are not sufficiently familiar with some of their writings. I will refer briefly to aspects of the contribution of Hume, Linnaeus, Blumenbach and Cuvier, adding brief comments on three Britons – Charles White, Thomas Carlyle and Robert Knox.

Noted British philosopher David Hume claimed that people who lived in the South 'are inferior to the rest of the species and are incapable of higher attainment of the human mind'.[45] Although he did not support slavery, which, according to his utilitarian calculus, was not advantageous to the overall happiness of humankind, Hume had little respect for Blacks, whom he described in the following words: 'You may obtain anything of the NEGROES by offering them strong drink; and may easily prevail upon them to sell, not only their children, but their wives and mistresses, for a case of brandy.'[46]

In a footnote appearing in one of his works, Hume said, 'There never was a civilized nation of any complexion than white', and he opined that 'In Jamaica, indeed, they talk of one Negro as a man of parts and learning, but 'tis likely he is admired for very slender accomplishments like a parrot, who speaks a few words plainly.'[47] Hume attempted damage control when criticized for this claim; he revised the footnote containing the claim before he died. He stated instead that he was 'apt to suspect the negroes to be naturally inferior to the whites' and that 'There scarcely ever was a civilized nation of that [Black] complexion, nor even any individual eminent either in action or speculation.'[48]

Britain produced Charles White, the physician who founded the Manchester Royal Infirmary and who, in 1799, described white people as 'the most beautiful of the human race'. Claiming that whites were the 'most removed from brute creation', White said, 'No one will doubt [the] superiority' of white people.[49]

Over the years, many other well-known figures helped promote the idea of white people as superior to Blacks. In 1849, in an address to those he deemed his 'philanthropic friends', Scottish historian Thomas Carlyle[50] spelt out what he called his 'painful duty' to remind them of the estate of Blacks who, in his opinion, were created with the endowments to make them fit to serve their white European masters. 'Idle black people' in the West Indies, he said,

Have the right ... to be *compelled* to work as he was fit, and to *do* the Maker's will, who had constructed him with such and such prefigurements of capability. And I incessantly pray Heaven, all men, the whitest alike, and the blackest, the richest and the poorest, in other regions of the world, had attained precisely the same right, the divine right of being compelled (if 'permitted' will not answer) to do what work they are appointed for, and not to go idle another minute, in a life so short![51]

In 1850, British anatomist Robert Knox[52] argued passionately for the superiority of white people over especially Black people. 'With me,' he said, 'race, or hereditary descent, is everything; it stamps the man ... The races of men ... differ from each other widely – most widely.' '[T]he races of men are not the result of accident; they are not convertible into each other by any contrivance whatsoever. The eternal laws of nature must prevail.' 'Look all over the globe,' he said, 'it is always the same; the dark races stand still, the fair progress.' 'I feel disposed to think that there must be a physical, and consequently, a psychological inferiority in the dark races generally ... [owing to] perhaps specific characters in the quality of the brain itself.'[53] Knox concluded that the 'black races' cannot become civilized. 'Their future history must resemble the past. The Saxon race will never tolerate them.'[54] Black people are different from white people 'in everything as much as in colour'. 'The races of men when carefully examined will be found to show remarkable organic differences.'[55]

Whatever may be the disparate estimates of the contribution of each of the persons we have mentioned, hardly is there any doubt concerning Carl Linnaeus's significant contribution to the attempt to predicate racism on the foundation of science.

It was no less a person than the Swiss philosopher Jean-Jacques Rousseau who sent the following message to the Swedish scientist Linnaeus: 'Tell him I know no greater man on earth.'[56] Linnaeus had developed a taxonomy[57] that included categories of species with white Europeans at the top and Black Africans at the bottom of the human species. In this taxonomy, which, perhaps, still commands its band of supporters today, Linnaeus adopted a fourfold categorization of people as follows:

Homo Europeaeus, having white skin and identified as gentle and governed by laws.

Homo Americanus, with red skin and said to be choleric (irritable and easily angered) and governed by customs.

Homo Asiaticus, with yellow skin and described as haughty and governed by opinion.

Homo Afer, with black skin and characterized as indolent and governed by caprice.[58]

What Linnaeus attempted was a scientific taxonomy in which skin colour and behavioural characteristics were alleged to be related biologically. His theory provided what he considered a scientific foundation for classifying people. It provided the bedrock on which scientific racism was erected. On this foundation, deemed respectable by the unsuspecting, the edifice of evil that racism represents found final form.

With the passage of time, the study of 'race' that Linnaeus

started was to mushroom. In 1795, in the third edition of his work *On the Natural Varieties of Mankind*,[59] the German Johann Blumenbach identified five varieties of humankind: the Caucasian or white race; the Mongolian or yellow race; the Malayan or brown race; the Ethiopian or Black race; and the American or red race. At first, Blumenbach held that '[T]he white color holds the first place', with people of other skin colour being mere degenerates of the original.[60] Eventually, he attributed skin colour to geography and diet, and he concluded that Africans belong to the human family and are not inferior to the other so-called races. In other words, Blumenbach did not claim that the classification system he developed was immutable.[61]

In the nineteenth century, the French zoologist Jean Léopold Cuvier, sometimes referred to as Georges Cuvier, reduced Blumenbach's race classification from five to three: Caucasian, comprising white people, with Adam and Eve as their progenitor in what Cuvier claimed was the original race; Mongolian – yellow people; and Ethiopians – Black people. Blacks, he said, were 'the most degraded of human races, whose form approaches that of the beast and whose intelligence is nowhere great enough to arrive at regular government'.[62] It took many years for the scientific community to effectively expose the pseudo-science that was used to justify white people subjugating Black people and to provide a bulwark against the advance of the march towards emancipation from slavery and the humanization of slaveholders.

Debunking the Myth of Biological Race

In the post-Enlightenment period, in which the idea of race achieved full expression as an ideology, many people subscribed to 'the claim that there [are] immutable major divisions of humankind, each with biologically transmitted characteristics'.[63] Each race was deemed 'a homogeneous group of individuals biologically or linguistically similar to one another and systematically distinguishable' from other so-called races.[64] Over time, the prevailing opinion on race became markedly different from what it was in the seventeenth and eighteenth centuries.

In the aftermath of the First World War, a Peace Conference was convened in Paris, which was expected to herald a new world order rising from the ash heap created by the war. Some participants hoped the conference would affirm the principle of equality among people deemed to belong to different racial groupings. However, the contributions of significant white delegates underlined the firm resolve of certain nations, especially Britain, the USA, South Africa and Australia, to maintain the principle of racial inequality.

The British representative, Harold Nicholson, baulked at any suggestion that 'implied the equality of the yellow man with the white man', not to mention what he termed 'the terrific theory of the equality of the white man with the black'.[65] British Prime Minister Lloyd George – a professed Baptist to boot – made an impassioned plea for France not to train what he termed 'big nigger armies'.[66] In the end, it took US President Woodrow Wilson to ensure the derailment of the intention of the majority on the League of Nations Commission to affirm 'the principle of equality of nations and just treatment of nationals'.[67]

When, in 1948, the United Nations issued the International Declaration of Human Rights, the groundwork was laid for the further undermining of the assumptions informing the ideology of race and the practice of racism. Two years later, the United Nations Educational, Scientific and Cultural Organization (UNESCO) issued a *Statement on Race*,[68] declaring:

Scientists have reached general agreement in recognizing that mankind is one; that all men [*sic*] belong to the same species, homo sapiens.

For all practical social purposes, 'race' is not so much a biological phenomenon as a social myth ... [that] has created an enormous amount of social damage.

As more and more people began to agree that racism was inconsistent with respect for human rights, the UN General Assembly, in 1963, approved a resolution affirming the Declaration on the

Elimination of All Forms of Racial Discrimination. According to that declaration, 'any doctrine of racial differentiation or superiority is scientifically false, morally condemnable, socially unjust and dangerous, and ... there is no justification for racial discrimination either in theory or in practice'.[69]

In 1965, the UN adopted and opened for signature and ratification the International Convention on the Elimination of All Forms of Racial Discrimination. A year later, an International Day for the Elimination of Racial Discrimination was designated. By 1967, UNESCO gave fuller expression to its understanding of race in a *Statement on Race and Racial Prejudice*.[70] A UNESCO committee of experts from 17 countries declared:

- All men [*sic*] living today belong to the same species and descend from the same stock.
- Current biological knowledge does not permit us to impute cultural achievements to differences in genetic potential.
- Racism falsely claims that there is a scientific basis for arranging groups hierarchically in terms of psychological and cultural characteristics that are immutable and innate.

During the 1970s, the UN General Assembly adopted the International Convention on the Suppression and Punishment of the Crime of Apartheid. It also declared 1973–82 as the Decade for Action to Combat Racism and Racial Discrimination. The hope was that the period would be used for concrete action to eliminate the evils it identified. Needless to say, at the end of the decade, little had changed in attitudes to race. Not surprisingly, therefore, subsequently the UN found it necessary to declare a second, and later a third, Decade for Action to Combat Racism and Racial Discrimination – 1983–92 and 1994–2003, respectively.

During this third decade, certain groups within the scientific community made significant decisions to register their rejection of the ideology of race. Take, for example, the Statement on 'Race' issued in 1998 by the American Anthropological Association. It explicitly states:

With the vast expansion of scientific knowledge ... it has become clear that human populations are not unambiguous,
clearly demarcated, biologically distinct groups ... Given
what we know about the capacity of normal humans to
achieve and function within any culture, we conclude that
present-day inequalities between so-called 'racial' groups are
not consequences of their biological inheritance but products
of historical and contemporary social, economic, educational,
and political circumstances.[71]

The UN convened World Conferences to Combat Racism
and Racial Discrimination. The first took place in Geneva in
1978, and the second in Durban, South Africa, in 2001. The
Conference Statement[72] produced by the Second World Conference against Racism, Racial Discrimination, Xenophobia
and Related Intolerance reaffirmed customary principles earlier
adumbrated. Notably, it recognized

with grave concern that, despite the efforts of the international community, the principal objectives of the three Decades
to Combat Racism and Racial Discrimination [had] not been
attained and that countless human beings [continued] to the
present day to be victims of racism, racial discrimination,
xenophobia and related intolerance.

The Conference affirmed that

racism, racial discrimination, xenophobia and related intolerance, where they amount to racism and racial discrimination,
constitute serious violations of, and obstacles to, the full
enjoyment of all human rights and deny the self-evident truth
that all human beings are born free and equal in dignity and
rights, and are among the root causes of many internal and
international conflicts ... and the consequent forced displace-
ment of populations.

Firmly 'rejecting any doctrine of racial superiority, along with
theories that attempt to determine the existence of so-called

distinct human races', and reaffirming that 'all peoples and individuals constitute one human family, rich in diversity', the Conference emphasized the need for 'a global fight against racism, racial discrimination, xenophobia and related intolerance and all their abhorrent and evolving forms and manifestations' and called this 'a matter of priority for the international community'. The Conference also proposed a programme of action designed to address the scourge of racism that continues to be evident today.

Since that conference, further action has been taken in the scientific community to help consolidate the gains contingent upon the rejection of the alleged scientific foundation for the idea of a firm link between biology and 'race'. In 2011, the International Union of Anthropological and Ethnological Sciences issued its own Statement on Race and Racism in which it declared:

All humans living today belong to a single species, Homo sapiens, and share a common descent. All living human populations have evolved from one common ancestral group over the same period of time.

For centuries, scholars have sought to comprehend patterns in nature by classifying living things. Attempts to classify human populations in this manner have been wholly misplaced ... [H]umanity cannot be classified into discreet geographical categories on the basis of biological differences.

There is no necessary concordance between biological characteristics and culturally defined groups.

Eloise Meneses,[73] in her succinct summary of the basis of the rejection of the pseudoscience of race, presents three postulates. First, 'human beings as a whole constitute a very narrow gene pool ... [O]ther species have far more variation than [humans] do.' Second, 'most of the physical variation that does exist [among humans] is spread throughout the entire human population' and is not characteristic of any specific group within the population. Third, 'slight variations between populations do not indicate race lines. [Humans] are all genetically related. There are no pure stocks among us; nor have there ever been in the past.' Meneses concludes that 'in the biological world', 'there is no such thing, nor has there ever been', such a thing 'as race'.[74]

The alleged scientific basis for the notion of biological race has been rejected by most scientists, sociologists and anthropologists, many of whom have helped clarify that race is a socially constructed identity. It does not correspond to any set of biological features that were once used as a basis for dividing humankind into different racial groupings. It is now generally affirmed that biologically there is only one race – the human race. And the 'races' we have reified are social constructs that are not based on biology but represent a strategy of dominant ethnic groups that wish to assert their superiority over others. The existence of so-called 'races' is highly contested.

Not surprisingly, when the World Council of Churches deliberated on the subject of race and racism at its fourth assembly in 1968 – and the Council did this in the context of the discussion on race that was taking place in the international community – it identified the features of racism as follows:

• Ethnocentric pride in one's own racial group.
• Preference for the [alleged] distinguishing characteristics of that group.
• Belief that these group characteristics are fundamentally biological in nature and are transmitted to succeeding generations.
• Strong negative feelings towards other groups who do not share the defining characteristics of their group.
• Efforts to discriminate against and exclude the outgroup from full participation in the life of the community.[75]

Unfortunately, all the clarifying statements about race have not succeeded in eliminating the problem of racism. Not surprisingly, therefore, we are focusing on the subject of race in this lecture. Because racism is a problem as much within the church community as outside of it, I end this lecture with some action items that are grounded in the faith of the church that could revolutionize the way the church deals with the subject of race. Deconstructing the notion of race and, animated by the renewed commitment to implement the action items that I will identify, the church may register further progress on the road to truly loving others following the pattern Jesus has taught and exemplified.

Looking Towards the Future

The association of biology and race constitutes the very foundation of the problem of race and racist ideology. This ideology is a human creation designed both to make inequality between people appear to be inborn and to reinforce the belief that it is part of the taken-for-granted landscape of human life. If Christians today are to come to terms with the serious problem reflected in the popular understanding of race, some important steps need to be taken. I mention briefly four of these steps that are rooted in a Trinitarian framework that issues into what I regard as a responsible theological anthropology. In light of these, I will suggest that the churches initiate a specific action to help them overcome their apathy on issues of race.

First, the church needs to expose a fundamental misunderstanding of the divine nature that undergirds the ideology of race. This is the error of segregating human freedom from its foundation and grounding in divine freedom. God, by whose own volition the world was created and in whose providence human beings are entrusted with the stewardship of creation, has endowed humankind with the gift of freedom. In sovereign freedom, God bestows liberty on human beings whom God has made, and God wills that that liberty be respected. The denial of the freedom that rightly belongs to each human being represents a rejection of the divine design for creation. As Noel Erskine has said, 'Whenever the church fails to make the connection between divine freedom and human freedom, it supports and gives its blessings to vicious structures of oppression in our world.'[76]

Commenting on the biblical narrative of creation, Dwight Hopkins has explained that 'God breathed the Spirit of liberation, the Spirit to be free, into the very act of creation itself

... (Gen 2.7).'[77] The freedom each human being receives is 'the freedom inherent in God's own self'.[78] The gift of freedom entails freedom

> to enjoy all of God's work without ... external negative restraints of any kind. In sum, human beings were brought into existence to be in equal relationship at each stage of their interactions ... God implanted liberation in the created human beings [so that] this liberation may be enacted on the everyday and ordinary levels of existence.[79]

To deny human beings the capacity to freely exercise their liberty is to fly in the face of the Creator, who is the giver of freedom. The church needs to rediscover and acknowledge the link between divine freedom and human freedom and place this link at the centre of its discourse on what it means to be a part of the creation that God has made.

Second, Christians may need to intentionally re-engage the Christocentric faith that highly values what God has accomplished for the salvation of the world through the sacrifice of Christ. This is an important requirement if we are to come to terms with, and to develop the resolve to work consistently to overcome, the serious problem that inheres in a biological understanding of 'race'. When we allow our God-given freedom to be contaminated by distorted understandings, false pride or the pursuit of power, sin is at work in humankind. When, through his life, death and resurrection, Jesus Christ secures victory over sin, God swings the door wide open for the renewal and reinvigoration of what it means to be truly human. God enables people to see the self and the other as equally valid expressions of God's mysterious action in creation and redemption. Then, the way of the follower of Christ will reflect the grammar of that mutual respect and *agape* love that are perfectly inhospitable to any claim of the inherent superiority of one person over another. Our Christocentric faith derives from Christ's action in breaking down the walls that separate people from one another, releasing them for the wholesome enjoyment of *ubuntu*.

In a White Paper on Welfare, the South African government in 1996 expressed its understanding of *ubuntu* in the following terms. *Ubuntu* is

> The principle of caring for each other's well-being ... and a spirit of mutual support ... Each individual's humanity is ideally expressed through his or her relationship with others and theirs in turn through a recognition of the individual's humanity. Ubuntu means that people are people through other people. It also acknowledges both the rights and the responsibilities of every citizen in promoting individual and societal well-being.[80]

In the perspective of *ubuntu*, a Trinitarian Christocentric faith will not accommodate the negative images of others and of otherness that we create and utilize as identity markers that serve to galvanize our feelings of superiority over others. Instead, we will assign to each – and to all persons – the primary identity of a human being. With fellow Christians, we will affirm our shared identity in Jesus Christ.

People have an incredible capacity for inventing identities for groups of people belonging to other cultures. We call them barbarians, savages, infidels, pagans, heathens, unenlightened children, aboriginals, or natives, and we construct these identities in order to maintain dominance over them in patronizing ways. With a truly Christocentric faith, we are capable of imagining how human diversity finds a safe home within the one mystical body of Christ where no one is demeaned or disrespected and all who confess Christ are welcome at the table of life.[81]

It is supremely in Jesus Christ, who is the icon of the invisible God, that one sees the full manifestation of the freedom bequeathed to all Christians. This freedom is marked by self-emptying love – the love that reaches out for the sake of the beloved rather than as part of a utilitarian game pursued in search of personal honour, glory or 'success'. The selfless love that is part and parcel of our response to Christ is a strategy to secure the liberation of creation. Christocentric faith opens up

space for covenantal partnerships geared towards the edifica-
tion of all and aimed at the welfare of the whole community.

Third, a vital need exists for the rediscovery of the pneuma-
tological dimensions of faithful Christian living. Only so will
the church be ready to appropriate the power to discern the
ways in which sin is at work in the structures and arrangements
that serve the cause of human domination.

The Holy Spirit opens our understanding to our vocational
obligation to live with the symphony of existential relatedness
with God and with other human beings within the community
of the whole creation. Enlivened by the Holy Spirit, human
beings discern the contours of what Barbara Trepagnier calls
'silent racism' – the unspoken racist thoughts and unacknow-
ledged racist assumptions that inform the attitudes many people
display and that inform the stereotypes we invent and the institutions we develop.[82]

The Spirit alone can cleanse our minds enabling us to understand ways in which many of us are beneficiaries of institutional
racism, which, whether we like it or not, makes us complicit in
the sin from whose perpetration we continue to reap privileges
and benefits. It is the Holy Spirit who will help us detect what
Charles Mills calls *The Racial Contract* that is presupposed by
the social contractarianism that informs and is implicit in much
of our contemporary political discourse and arrangements.[83]

Jürgen Moltmann caught a glimpse of the freedom the Holy
Spirit brings when he referred to the church as 'a fellowship of
the free'. It is 'an order of freedom' in which, as he said, 'people
are freed from the oppression which separates them from others'
and frees them 'for free fellowship with one another'.[84] In this
community, the negative identities we construct for ourselves
and for others cannot stand in the light of the new reality God
calls the church to unveil before the world. In this reality, each
person appears as a child of God with the heritage of that freedom that is given in Christ. As a community living under the
reign of Christ, where the pernicious forces of this world have
been undermined and the cruel powers dethroned, the church
becomes, in the words of Moltmann, 'the fellowship of Christ
through faith and hope, discipleship and new fellowship' mani-

festing what it means to be freed by Christ. A rediscovery both of the place of the Holy Spirit in the life of Christ-followers and of the process of sanctification in a believer's life is of vital importance for the living out of the loving relations that should characterize the Christian community.

Fourth, contemporary Christians need to read the Bible with eyes wide open so as to be able to discern, against the grain of some dominant readings, the radical importance of the creation of humankind in the image of God. The living out of the faith on the bedrock of an informed and defensible theological anthropology is the *sine qua non* of genuine Christian discipleship. By reading the Scriptures in the key of this rounded theological anthropology that 'interrogates what people are created and called to be and to do',[85] several challenges may be met and overcome.

First, one will be disposed to reject the heretical claims regarding the enslavement of Black people as just payment for the sin of Ham.[86] Second, one's approach will thoroughly undermine the claims of those who make the Creator culpable for the racist ideology that denies the equal dignity of all human beings created by the one God. Racists accomplish this by claiming that the instinct to regard others as inferior to oneself is consistent with divine providence. This applies especially to white people who are inheritors of what Caroline Redfearn describes as 'the theological racism that humanity was originally White'.[87] Third, those who read Scripture through the lens of a mature theological anthropology will be led to identify with the thoroughgoing critique of social injustice in the tradition of the great prophets of ancient Israel and to embrace, with joyful abandon, Jesus' ethic of radical love of neighbour. As J. Kameron Carter has pointed out, Christ's followers need to engage the creative theological imagination that makes possible a reading of Scripture 'against, rather than within, the social order'.[88] When this way of reading Scripture is pursued, the sharp edges of the dagger of racism will be rendered useless against the bedrock of informed faith.

In the light of all that has been said, may I assert that perhaps we now need to determine whether a *status confessionis* has arrived in relation to any church congregation that denies that racism is a sin, that refuses to affirm that those Christians who practise and defend it are compromising their standing in Christ, and that refrains from taking concrete and decisive action to root out racism from its life. By not participating in the struggle to overcome racism, such a congregation has turned its back on the truth of the gospel and has become a pseudo-church.

It was in his profound disappointment with the church under Nazi Germany, and more specifically with the watering down of the first draft of the Bethel Confession,[89] that Dietrich Bonhoeffer called attention to *status confessionis*. This idea refers to the existence of a situation that threatens to destroy the integrity of the church's confession of faith. Such a situation demands a restatement of the faith that inevitably includes a distinction between 'true' and 'false' church.[90]

By invoking the *status confessionis*, the church declares that Christians and churches defending a position that is profoundly unchristian are guilty of heresy. This means that the ecclesial proponents and defenders of seriously flawed socio-political and ethical beliefs are seen to be disqualifying themselves from participation in the wider family of Christ's church. They can no longer be regarded as churches in the true sense because they have forsaken and are living in corporate betrayal of the true gospel and its just demands.[91]

At least two Christian world communions applied the concept of *status confessionis* in their relation to apartheid. The Lutheran World Federation (LWF) took this action in 1977, and the World Alliance (now World Communion) of Reformed Churches (WCRC) did the same in 1982.[92] This development was occasioned by the crisis created by the attitude of certain churches to apartheid. Through their support and defence of institutional racism, the Dutch Reformed Church in South Africa, for example, jeopardized the integrity of the Gospel and rejected solidarity with the body of Christ.[93]

I urge that the drastic action of declaring that a *status confessionis* has arrived in relation to certain churches, that is, certain church congregations, is needed in our times. National ecclesial communions need to declare a *status confessionis* in relation to their member churches, that is, their member con-gregations that practise racism and endorse racist ideology. The reason I make this appeal is that the problem of racism has proved to be intractable. The responsiveness of sections of the church community to the ubiquity of racism has been sluggish. Ecclesial inaction, in the face of the religious, social, political and economic consequences of racism, has devas-tating consequences for the witness of the church and the integrity of the gospel it preaches. The inaction of some church congregations is too disastrous to be ignored. Every congrega-tion has an obligation to play its part in loosening the mortar cementing the brickwork of prejudice and hate. Drastic action needs to be taken that obliges each church congregation to take a stand, and that warns every ecclesial congregation of the inadmissible compromise that is inherent in inaction on the racism front.

Perhaps, the four steps I have identified and the suggestion I have made for the church's resolute action against racism will not adequately respond to Willie Jennings' call for a radical transformation of the Christian imagination that would evince a reconfiguration of living spaces into locations where people can imagine new ways of connecting with each other and desire new patterns of social joining. I hope, however, that what I have suggested would contribute to that understanding of life together that is consistent with the church's vision of the kingdom of God.[94]

Should the deconstruction of our racialized world view be achieved, it will be possible for the churches to develop the capacity to envision a new social order in which inequalities based on assumptions of 'race' no longer prevail within the ecclesial community. It will be possible for the churches to exhibit their commitment to realize in themselves, in others and in our world the joy of loving as Jesus did, of sharing and caring as Jesus did, and of bearing compelling witness to life in community marked by oneness with Christ. Then, churches will launch out into a world in which all people, created in the image of God, may learn from them not only how to live in peace with justice but also how to engage in fierce competition to outdo one another in showing honour and extending a hand of selfless love to each other.

Notes

1 Aristotle, *Politics*, Book 1, Part 5, in *Social and Political Philosophy: Readings from Plato to Gandhi* (1963), ed. John Somerville and Ronald Santoni, New York: Anchor Books, pp. 64, 65. Ivan Hannaford has claimed that Aristotle's ideas on slavery have been 'grossly misinterpreted and overplayed'. He believes that generations of scholars have attributed to the Greeks and Romans racial attitudes they did not possess. See his (1996), *Race: The History of an Idea in the West*, Washington, DC: The Woodrow Wilson Center Press, especially Part II. Cf. Benjamin Isaac's assignment of the designation 'proto-racism' to forms of prejudice in classical antiquity. See his (2004), *The Invention of Racism in Classical Antiquity*, Princeton, NJ: Princeton University Press, and his essay 'Racism: A Rationalization of Prejudice in Greece and Rome', in *Origins of Racism in the West*, ed. Miriam Eliav-Feldon, Benjamin Isaac and Joseph Ziegler (2009), Cambridge: Cambridge University Press, pp. 32–56.

2 Euripides, *Iphigenia in Aulis*, 1400–01, available at: http://classics.mit.edu/Euripides/iphi_aul.html (accessed 9.6.23).

3 On Marcus Garvey's life, see, for example, Lewis, Rupert and Bryan, Patrick (1994), *Garvey: His Work and Impact*, Trenton: Africa World Press; Garvey, Amy (ed.) (1986), *The Political Philosophy and Opinions of Marcus Garvey or Africa for the Africans*, Dover, MA: The Majority Press; Blaisdell, Bob (ed.) (2004), *Selected Writings and Speeches of Marcus Garvey*, Dover, MA: Dover Publications.

4 *Declaration to the Word* by the Second Pan-African Congress of 1921, cited in DuBois, William E. B. (1964), *The World and Africa*, New York: International Publishers, p. 238.

5 Meneses, Eloise H. (2007), 'Science and the Myth of Biological Race', in *This Side of Heaven: Race, Ethnicity, and Christian Faith*, ed. Robert Priest and Alvaro Nieves, New York: Oxford University Press, p. 35.

6 Hirschman, Charles (2004), 'The Origins and Demise of the Conception of Race', *Population and Development Review* 30.(2), p. 401, cited in Eliav-Feldon, Isaac and Ziegler (eds), *Origins of Racism in the West*, pp. 7–8.

7 Lauren, Paul Gordon (1988), *Power and Prejudice: The Politics and Diplomacy of Racial Discrimination*, Boulder, CO: Westview, pp. 63–4.

8 Ferguson, Niall (2003), *Empire: The Rise and Demise of the Brit-*

ish World Order and the Lessons for Global Power, New York: Basic Books.

9 Cited in Parrillo, Vincent (2002), *Understanding Race and Ethnic Relations*, Boston, MA: Allyn and Bacon, p. 17; *Cicero, Letters to Atticus with an English Translation by E.O. Winstedt, MA, of Magdalen College, Oxford*, London: William Heinemann Ltd and Cambridge, MA: Harvard University Press, 1918.

10 Cited in Flynn, James (1980), *Race, IQ and Jansen*, London: Routledge & Kegan Paul, p. 217.

11 In the aftermath of the Second World War, many students from the Caribbean travelled to Britain to further their studies. Eugenia Charles, Michael Manley, Milton Cato and Errol Barrow, future Prime Ministers in the Caribbean, were among them. Also among them were future outstanding UWI professors such as Douglas Hall, Michael Smith, Roy Augier and Lloyd Braithwaite. See Gladstone Mills, 'Foreword' to Braithwaite, Lloyd (2001), *Colonial West Indian Students in Britain*, Mona: University of the West Indies Press, pp. vi–xii.

12 Snelgrave, William (1754), *A New Account of Some Parts of Guinea and the Slave Trade*, London: James, John and Paul Knapton, pp. 160–1, cited in Eric William (1964), *Capitalism and Slavery*, London: Andre Deutsch, p. 50.

13 Williams, *Capitalism and Slavery*, pp. 81–2.

14 Williams, *Capitalism and Slavery*, p. 82.

15 Donnan, Elizabeth (ed.) (1930–35), *Documents Illustrative of the History of the Slave Trade in America*, Washington, DC: Carnegie Institute of Washington, II, p. 609, cited in Williams, *Capitalism and Slavery*, p. 84.

16 See Rogers, Charles (ed.) (1876), *Boswelliana: The Commonplace Book of J. Boswell, with a Memoir and Annotations*, London: The Grampian Club, p. 116.

17 From Boswell's 1791 poem 'No Abolition of Slavery; or the Universal Empire of Love'. See Wood, Marcus (ed.) (2003), *The Poetry of Slavery: An Anglo-American Anthology, 1764–1865*, Oxford: Oxford University Press, p. 193. Interestingly, in *Busha's Mistress*, said to be a fictional book, an enslaved woman named Catherine replied to an invitation to return home in the following words: 'De grave is de home for such as we.' See Shepherd, Verene (2007), '"Petticoat Rebellion"?: Women in Emancipation', in *Emancipation: The Lessons and the Legacy*, ed. Hopeton Dunn, Kingston: Arawak Publications, p. 120.

18 Lauren, *Power and Prejudice*, p. 91.

19 Lauren, *Power and Prejudice*, p. 102.

20 Perhaps the most comprehensive bibliography on Sam Sharpe is available in Reid-Salmon, Delroy (2012), *Burning for Freedom: A Theology of the Black Atlantic Struggle for Liberation*, Kingston: Ian Randle Publishers.

21 No one really knows how many Africans were transported from their continent for enslavement in the Caribbean and the Americas. Hugh Thomas (1997), *The Slave Trade: The Story of the Atlantic Slave Trade, 1440–1870*, New York: Touchstone, estimates that, between 1492 and 1870, the number was some 11 million. Basil Davidson (1980), in *The African Slave Trade: A Revised and Expanded Edition*, Boston, MA: Little, Brown, pp. 95–100 (+271), suggests the estimated number was 20 million. Walter Rodney estimates that 15 million enslaved Africans reached the American continent and the Caribbean, but suggests that, adding those killed in Africa in the process of obtaining people for enslavement and those who died on board the slave ships when crossing the Atlantic ocean, the numbers are more likely 40–50 million. (See his (1967), *West Africa and the Atlantic Slave Trade*, Dar es Salaam: East African Publishing House, p. 6.) It appears that the figure of 15 million is increasingly being found to be acceptable among many researchers.

22 Beckles, Hilary and Shepherd, Verene (2007), *Trading Souls: Europe's Transatlantic Trade in Africans, A Bicentennial Caribbean Reflection*, Kingston: Ian Randle Publishers, p. xxii, cited in Cawley, Bolt (2011), 'The Slave Trade and the Unholy Triangle: A Caribbean Perspective', in *Baptist Faith and Witness Book 4*, ed. Fausto Vasconcelos, Falls Church: Baptist World Alliance, p. 49.

23 Bleby, Henry (1853), *Death Struggles of Slavery: Being a Narrative of Facts and Incidents, Which Occurred in a British Colony, During the Two Years Immediately Preceding Negro Emancipation*, London: Hamilton, Adams, p. 118, cited in Lawson, Winston (1996), *Religion and Race: African and European Roots in Conflict – A Jamaican Testament*, New York: Peter Lang, p. 159.

24 *The Baptist Reporter*, July 1864, p. 305, cited in Dick, Devon (2009), *The Cross and Machete: Native Baptists of Jamaica*, Kingston: Ian Randle Publishers, p. 106.

25 From the *Belmore Papers*, cited in Dick, *The Cross and the Machete*, pp. 106–7.

26 Reid-Salmon, *Burning for Freedom*.

27 See St Clair, William (2007), *The Door of No Return: The History of the Cape Coast Castle and the Atlantic Slave Trade*, New York: Blue-Bridge. Earlier, the book appeared in the UK as (2006) *The Grand Slave Emporium*, London: Profile Books.

28 On the Castle, see St Clair, *The Door of No Return*.

29 Barry Higman explains how the slaveholders included enslaved persons, livestock and machines in their inventory. Barry Higman (1995), *Slave Population and Economy in Jamaica, 1807–1834*, Barbados, Jamaica, Trinidad and Tobago: The University Press, pp. 1–5. Orlando Patterson has refused to identify commodification as the defining mark of slavery, preferring loss of freedom as the primary index. See his (1982), *Slavery and Social Death: A Comparative Study*, Cambridge,

MA, and London: Harvard University Press. At his death, the jury estimated Sam Sharpe's value at £16.10. See Reid, C. S. (1988), *Samuel Sharpe: From Slave to National Hero*, Kingston: Bustamante Institute of Public Affairs.

30 William Knibb, British Parliamentary Papers, XX (721), 246, cited in Braithwaite, *Colonial West Indian Students*, p. 15.

31 See Callam, Neville (1998), 'Hope: A Caribbean Perspective', *Ecumenical Review* 50(2), April, pp. 137–42.

32 *Scenes in the Caribbean Sea: Being Sketches from a Missionary's Notebook* (London, 1854), p. 51, cited in Dick, *The Cross and the Machete*, p. 107.

33 Reid-Salmon, Delroy (2010), 'Faith and the Gallows: The Cost of Liberation', in *Black Theology, Slavery and Contemporary Christianity*, ed. Anthony Reddie, Surrey and Vermont: Ashgate Publishing, pp. 151–65.

34 Reid-Salmon, 'Faith and the Gallows', p. 153.

35 See, for example, Patterson, Orlando (1991), *Freedom in the Making of Western Culture*, New York: Basic Books. Heuman, Gad and Burnard, Trevor (eds) (2011), *The Routledge History of Slavery*, New York: Routledge; and the four-volume history of slavery published by Cambridge University Press in 2011 and 2012 as the *Cambridge World History of Slavery*. Volume 1 deals with the Ancient Mediterranean World; Volume 2, AD 500–1420; Volume 3, AD 1420–1804; Volume 4, 1804–2000.

36 For the brief discussion on the evolution of slavery in Europe, we draw extensively on two works: Hart, Richard (1980), *Slaves who Abolished Slavery*, Volume 1, *Blacks in Bondage*, Kingston: Institute of Social and Economic Research, University of the West Indies, pp. 1–20; Sweet, James (1997), 'The Iberian Roots of American Racist Thought', *William and Mary Quarterly* 51(1), January, pp. 143–66.

37 Sweet, 'The Iberian Roots', pp. 143–66.

38 Sweet, 'The Iberian Roots', pp. 145–6.

39 Hart, *Slaves who Abolished Slavery*, p. 19.

40 Patterson, Orlando (1982), *Slavery and Social Death: A Comparative Study*, Cambridge, MA, and London: Harvard University Press. Patterson characterizes slavery as an extreme form of 'personal domination', the enslaved being under the direct power of another. It represented a form of excommunication – the enslaved being denied independent social existence – with the enslaved being alienated from all rights and obligations related to their birth and their blood relations.

41 G. Gilbert to Governor. CO/137/155 (21 October 1823), 62, cited in Gosse, Dave St A., 'The Impact of the Haitian Revolution and Emancipation in Jamaica', in Hopeton Dunn (ed.) (2007), *Emancipation: The Lessons and the Legacy*, p. 183.

42 Hannaford, Ivan (1996), *Race: The History of an Idea in the West*, Washington, DC: The Woodrow Wilson Press, p. 187.

43 Sweet, 'The Iberian Roots', p. 165.

44 Patterson, *Slavery and Social Death*, p. 420.

45 'Of National Characters' 3.249 (1748), cited in Hannaford, *Race*, p. 215.

46 'Of National Characters' 3.257 (1748), cited in Hannaford, *Race*, p. 216.

47 Green, T. and Grose, T. (eds) (1886), 'Of National Characters', in *The Philosophical Works of David Hume, Volume 3*, London: Longmans, Green, p. 252. Also published as Hume, David (1777), *Essays and Treatises on Several Subjects*, in two volumes, London and Edinburgh, vol. 1, p. 550.

48 Whether or not Hume was responding to James Beattie's demolition of his claim concerning people who were not white (on this, see Aaron Garrett in his essay on 'Hume's Revised Racism' (*Hume Studies* XXVI, no. 1, April 2000, pp. 171–7), Hume never succeeded in denying he had expressed a racist opinion.

49 White, Charles (1799), *Regular Gradation of Man, and in Different Animals and Vegetables*, London: Dilly, p. 134, cited in Lauren, *Power and Prejudice*, p. 21.

50 'Occasional Discourses on the Negro Question', *Fraser's Magazine* 40, December 1849, pp. 670–9.

51 See Carlyle, Thomas (1888), *Thomas Carlyle's Works: Critical and Miscellaneous Essays*, London: Chapman and Hall; or Campbell, John (1951), Negromania: Being an Examination of the Falsely Assumed Equality of the Various Races of Men, Philadelphia, PA: Campbell and Power.

52 Knox, Robert (1850), *The Races of Man: A Fragment*, Philadelphia: Lea and Blanchard, 1850, accessible at: http://books.google.com/books?id=XwQXAAAAYAAJ&printsec=frontcover&source=gbs_ge_summary_r& cad=o#v=onepage&q&f=false (accessed 9.6.23).

53 Knox, *The Races of Man*, p. 151.

54 Knox, *The Races of Man*, p. 162.

55 Knox, *The Races of Man*, p. 10. Emphasis added.

56 See: https://www.botan.uu.se/learning/linnaeus-online/the-life-of-Linnaeus/carl-von-linne-the-nobleman/what-people-have-said-about-linnaeus/ (accessed 28.6.23).

57 See his (1735), *Systema Naturae*. On his pseudo-scientific contribution to the understanding of race, see, for example, Meneses, 'Science and the Myth of Biological Race', pp. 33–46.

58 In Hannaford's words, Linnaeus divided humankind into 'White European, Red American, Dark Asiatic, and Black Negro'. See his *Race*, p. 204.

59 Blumenbach, Johann (1795/1969), *On the Natural Varieties of*

Mankind: De Generis Humani Varietate Nativa, New York: Bergman, 1969 reprint.

60 Blumenbach, *On the Natural Varieties of Mankind*, p. 269, cited in Lauren, *Power and Prejudice*, p. 21.

61 See Hannaford, *Race*, pp. 207–13.

62 On Jean Cuvier, popularly called Georges Cuvier, see, for example, Gould, Stephen (1996), *The Mismeasure of Man*, New York: Norton and Co., pp. 63–74. See also Hannaford, *Race*, pp. 256–7.

63 Hannaford, *Race*, p. 17.

64 Hannaford, *Race*, p. 17.

65 Nicholson, Harold (1933), *Peacemaking, 1919*, Boston, MA: Houghton Mifflin Company, p. 145.

66 Lauren, *Power and Prejudice*, p. 106; Miller, David (1928), *The Drafting of the Covenant*, New York: Putnam, 1:116.

67 Lauren, *Power and Prejudice*, ch. 3. Thankfully, at the UN General Assembly meeting in Paris, December 1948, delegates were able to agree to work towards producing a Universal Declaration of Human Rights.

68 For the UNESCO statements on race, see UNESCO (1969), *Four Statements on the Race Question*, Paris: UNESCO. The text is available at: http://unesdoc.unesco.org/images/0012/001229/122962eo.pdf (accessed 9.6.23).

69 Preamble to the Declaration, whose full text was published by the United Nations in (1973), *Human Rights: A Compilation of International Instruments of the United Nations*, New York: United Nations, p. 22 and is widely available.

70 For the UNESCO statements on race, see UNESCO, *Four Statements*.

71 The Statement is available at: https://americananthro.org/about/policies/statement-on-race/ (accessed 29.6.23).

72 The text is available at: http://www.un.org/WCAR/durban.pdf (accessed 29.6.23)

73 Meneses, 'Science and the Myth of Biological Race', pp. 35–9. See also, for example, Unander, Dave (2000), *Shattering the Myth of Race: Genetic Realities and Biblical Truths*, Valley Forge, PA: Judson Press, pp. 43–61.

74 For a fuller exposition of the myth of biological race, see Kidd, Colin (2006), *The Forging of Races: Race and Scripture in the Protestant Atlantic World, 1600–2000*, Cambridge: Cambridge University Press, and Unander (2000), *Shattering the Myth of Race*.

75 Goodall, Norman (ed.) (1968), *The Uppsala Report 1968: Official Report of the Fourth Assembly of the World Council of Churches, Uppsala, July 4–20, 1968*, Geneva: WCC, p. 241.

76 Erskine, Noel (1981), *Decolonizing Theology: A Caribbean Perspective*, Maryknoll, NY: Orbis Books, p. 119. In a recent paper,

'Prophetic of Freedom Soon Come: Reflections on Sam Sharpe, Religion, Freedom and Jamaica at Fifty', Jamaican theologian Anna Perkins has emphasized the importance of 'enfleshing on social life' Sam Sharpe's 'religious ideal of freedom'. The paper was delivered at the Sam Sharpe Conference in Kingston on 1 December 2012.

77 Hopkins, Dwight (2000), *Down, Up and Over: Slave Religion and Black Theology*, Minneapolis, MN: Fortress Press, p. 239.

78 Hopkins, *Down, Up and Over*, p. 239.

79 Hopkins, *Down, Up and Over*, pp. 240–1.

80 *South African Government Gazette*, 2.2.1996. On *ubuntu*, see, for example, Tutu, Desmond (1999), *No Future without Forgiveness*, New York: Random House; Teffo, Joe (1994), *The Concept of Ubuntu as a Cohesive Moral Value*, Pretoria: Ubuntu School of Philosophy; Teffo, Joe (1994), *Towards a Conceptualization of Ubuntu*, Pretoria: Ubuntu School of Philosophy; Ndaba, W. J. (1994), *Ubuntu in Comparison to Western Philosophies*, Pretoria: Ubuntu School of Philosophy; Van Niekerk, Attie (1994), *Ubuntu and Religion*, Pretoria: Ubuntu School of Philosophy; Van Binsbergen, Wim (2001), 'Ubuntu and the Globalization of Southern African Thought and Society', *Quest: An African Journal of Philosophy* XV (1– 2), pp. 53–89; and Battle, Michael (1997), *Reconciliation: The Ubuntu Theology of Desmond Tutu*, Cleveland, OH: Pilgrim Press.

81 See Hiebert, Paul (2007), 'Western Images of Others and Otherness', in Priest and Nieves, *This Side of Heaven*, pp. 97–110.

82 Trepagnier, Barbara (2010), *Silent Racism: How Well-Meaning White People Perpetuate the Racial Divide*, expanded edn, Boulder, CO: Paradigm Publishers.

83 See Mills, Charles (1997), *The Racial Contract*, Ithaca, NY: Cornell University Press.

84 Moltmann, Jürgen (1975), *The Church in the Power of the Holy Spirit: A Contribution to the Messianic Ecclesiology*, San Francisco, CA: HarperCollins, pp. 291–4.

85 Hopkins, Dwight (2005), *Being Human: Race, Culture, and Religion*, Minneapolis, MN: Fortress Press, p. 161.

86 On this, see, for example: Goldenberg, David (2003), *The Curse of Ham: Race and Slavery in Early Judaism, Christianity and Islam*, Princeton, NJ: Princeton University Press; Glaney, Jennifer (2006), *Slavery in Early Christianity*, Minneapolis, MN: Fortress Press; McCall, Emanuel (2007), *When God's Children Get Together: A Memoir of Race*, Macon, GA: Mercer University Press. It is interesting to note that renowned international lawyer Hugo Grotius once stated: 'By the law of nature, in its primeval state, apart from human institutions and customs, no men can be slaves; and it is in this sense that legal writers maintain the opinion that slavery is repugnant to nature. Yet, in a former part of this treatise, it was shewn that there is nothing repugnant to natural

justice, in deriving the origin of servitude from human actions, whether founded upon compact or crime.' Grotius (1949), *De jure belli et pacis*, New York: Black, trans. Louise Loomis. See Book 2, ch. 5, and Book 3, ch. 7.

87 'A Legacy of Slavery – Black with the Slaves or Mulatto with the Slavers? An English Jamaican Theological Reflection on the Trajectories of "Mixed Race Categories"', in Reddie, Anthony (ed.) (2010), *Black Theology, Slavery and Contemporary Christianity*, Farnham: Ashgate, p. 140.

88 Carter, J. Kameron (2008), *Race: A Theological Account*, New York: Oxford University Press, p. 233.

89 This is the confession that was drafted in 1933 by Dietrich Bonhoeffer, Georg Merz, Hermann Sasse and others. It was an effort to confess the Christian faith in the midst of a situation when Christian solidarity with the Jewish people was seriously in question.

90 De Gruchy, John (2005), *Daring, Trusting Spirit: Bonhoeffer's Friend Eberhard Bethge*, Minneapolis, MN: Fortress Press, p. 9. See also De Gruchy, John and Villa-Vicencio, Charles (eds) (1983), *Apartheid is Heresy*, Grand Rapids, MI: William B. Eerdmans Publishing.

91 See, for example, Richardson, Neville (1986), 'Apartheid, Heresy and the Church in South Africa', *The Journal of Religious Ethics* 14(1), Spring, pp. 1–21; Henricksson, Lennart (2010), *A Journey with a Status Confessionis: Analysis of an Apartheid Related Conflict between the Dutch Reformed Church in South Africa and the World Alliance of Reformed Churches, 1982–1998*, Uppsala: Swedish Institute of Missionary Research; Hamann, Henry (c. 1985), 'Status Confessionis', in *A Lively Legacy: Essays in Honor of Robert Preus*, ed. Kurt E. Marquart, John R. Stephenson and Bjarne W. Teigen, Fort Wayne, IN: Concordia Theological Seminary, pp. 40 ff, also available at: www.ctsfw.net/media/pdfs/HamannApartheidandSTATUSCONFESSIONIS.pdf (accessed 10.6.23); and Lodberg, Peter (1996), 'Apartheid as a Church Dividing Issue', *The Ecumenical Review* 48(2), April, pp. 173–7. The notion of *status confessionis* has deep roots in the Reformation.

92 The LWF decision was made at their sixth assembly in Dar es Salaam, Tanzania, in June 1977 and the WARC's affirmation was issued at their General Council in Ottawa, Canada, in August 1982. At their Assembly in Debrecen, Hungary, in 1997, WARC had initiated a *processus confessionis* in a last push to educate the churches on such issues as economic justice prior to the declaration of a *status confessionis*.

93 See Roberts, J. Deotis (2005), *Bonhoeffer and King: Speaking Truth to Power*, Louisville, KY: Westminster John Knox Press, pp. 88–9. In 1956, 21 years before the LWF arrived at its decision, English Anglican bishop Trevor Huddleston had declared that 'racialism' in any form is an 'inherent blasphemy' against the nature of God who has created human beings in God's own image and that the Calvinism espoused

by the Dutch Reformed Church in South Africa as 'sub-Christian', 'like all heresies and deviations from Catholic truth ... is sub-Christian'. Huddleston, Trevor (1956), *Naught for Your Comfort*, Garden City, NY: Doubleday. Of course, from its inaugural Assembly in Amsterdam in 1948, the WCC had declared that 'Anti-semitism is sin against God and man'. This was an early indication that the ecumenical body would not be unwilling to declare itself in *status confessionis* with regard to a serious social issue with deep moral implications. See World Council of Churches Assembly (1949), *Man's Disorder and God's Design: The Amsterdam Assembly Series*, New York: Harper & Brothers; Gros, Jeffrey (1995), 'Eradicating Racism: A Central Agenda for the Faith and Order Movement', *Ecumenical Review* 47(1) January, pp. 42–51; McCullum, Hugh (2004), 'Racism and Ethnicity', in *A History of the Ecumenical Movement Volume 3, 1968–2000*, ed. John Briggs, Mercy Oduyoye and George Tsetsis, Geneva: WCC Publications, pp. 345–72. Since 2000, important developments on the racism front have taken place in the WCC, including significant work in Faith and Order, in the CWME, and through the Central Committee. WCC's official participation in the UN-sponsored World Conference against Racism, Racial Discrimination, Xenophobia and Related Intolerance in Durban, South Africa, in 2001, and the recent Doorn Conference in Utrecht, The Netherlands, in 2009, and in the 2010 Cleveland Conference on Racism Today express what appears to be a renewed effort to assert the WCC's seriousness regarding the problem of racism that persists despite all the efforts to overcome it.

94 See Jennings, Willie (2010), *The Christian Imagination: Theology and the Origins of Race*, New Haven, CT, and London: Yale University Press. Jennings alleges the replacement of race with a 'place and place-centered identity' that keeps 'renewing with each generation of race-formed children'. He does not believe the elimination of race is what is needed, but instead a new order in which boundary-defying relationships will mark the new living spaces created by a new order that hosts 'different ways of life that announce invitations for joining'.

9

Sam Sharpe: Deliver Us from Evil

Professor Robert Beckford, 2012

Introduction

'Deliver us from evil' is the third from last line in the Lord's Prayer in Matthew 6. Traditionally Black Pentecostals, like myself, were taught to read this passage as a literal prayer taught by Jesus to his disciples to be imitated by subsequent generations of followers throughout the ages. In recent years, however, many scholars have come to realize that the prayer is more of a political manifesto than a model Christian prayer. Within this new understanding, the prayer guides what the disciples of Jesus are to stand for. Hence, the reason why the disciples ask Jesus at the outset, 'What are we to pray for?' meaning, 'What are we to stand for?' As a manifesto for change, the call in the passage for 'daily bread' and 'forgiveness of debts' is a condemnation of the crippling effects of Roman rule and the collusion of the Jerusalem Temple elites. Likewise, 'deliver us from evil' is not a request for divine protection against demonic influence, but instead a plea for the spirituality and courage to never give up the struggle for justice in the world.

If we accept the Lord's Prayer as a manifesto for change rather than a traditional devotional resource, it becomes a powerful tool for a bottom-up struggle against injustice, especially powerful colonizing forces like the Roman Empire and their avaricious and rapacious intent.

For me, the life of Sam Sharpe, the Jamaican Baptist slave leader, exemplifies what it means to seek deliverance from evil *or* not opt out of the struggle for justice, but his example does not end on a note of moral courage. Instead, a closer inspection of the events after Christmas Day in Jamaica in 1831 provides us with precise details of *how* to resist tyranny.

In this lecture, I want to excavate the organizational prowess of Sam Sharpe as an integral feature of the Baptist War of 1831. This is because I believe Sharpe's community organizing to be the most dynamic and relevant aspect of the rebellion for successive generations of Jamaicans, its diaspora and those connected to the Baptist Christian tradition in Britain. To arrive at an understanding of Sharpe as an organizer, I want to begin by contouring the historical events of 1831 and afterwards identify some of the factors that have inhibited an activist transmission of this history. I will end by rereading the organization of the 1831 rebellion through the lenses of Saul Alinsky's 1970 classic text for community organizers, *Rules for Radicals*.[1]

Slaves No More – Background and Course of the Revolt

The Christmas holidays of 1831 in Jamaican slave society marks one of the most important historical moments in Caribbean history. On the evening of 27 December 1831, the burning of trash houses in the west of the island sent plumes of black smoke into the Caribbean evening skies and signalled the beginning of a slave revolt. It was the start of a sit-down protest by slaves in Jamaica that would transform the future of the island and the business of slavery. The rebellion, led by Sam Sharpe, involved between 20,000 and 45,000 slaves in rebellion against the British colonizers.

The background to the events is a long tradition of African-Jamaican resistance to slavery. Indeed, the liberation struggle against the transatlantic slave trade is divided into four basic stages. It begins with the captures and escapes of Africans during the period of forced capture in Africa and the middle passage and moves next to the plantation experience from the sixteenth to the late eighteenth century and the establishment of the plantation system in the Caribbean. Next it moves to the development of a wholly slave-based economy from the mid-eighteenth to the beginning of the nineteenth century, to the final period of crisis in the plantation system from 1800 to emancipation in 1834/38.

The motivation for this revolt was obvious: resistance to slavery. But what is not so obvious to us is the multivalent nature of slavery in the Caribbean. Slavery was never just an economic and social system – it was, for many of the slaves, a metaphysical reality. Indeed, in recent years, Charles Long, the great dean of African American Religious Studies, has taught religionists and theologians to think of the coming of the West on Africa and the New World in the age of European expansion as a spiritual activity that involved not only the breaking of flesh and bone but also the destruction of world view and cosmology. Thinking of slavery as a spiritual reality or mystical violence allows us to rethink how we conceptualize opposition to it. Thinking along these lines, opposition and resistance to slavery is, in Pentecostal speak, spiritual warfare. That is exorcising an occult practice. This image can be read back into slave history. It should be of no surprise, therefore, that the major revolts in Jamaica against slavery, including the Tacky rebellion of 1760 and also the Baptist War of 1831, have strong religious themes running through them. The Obeah-Myal complex and African-Jamaican Christianity run through the Tacky and Sam Sharpe revolts, respectively. As we shall see later, the religious reading of the rebellion is central to one of the major reinterpretations of the revolt.

Regarding the course of the events – why was Jamaica ripe for rebellion in 1831? Were there internal and external factors at work?

Two external factors may have prompted the slaves to revive the idea of an all-out revolt against the system since Tacky's revolt was brutally crushed. The first was the victory of slaves against the French colonial power in San Domingo and the establishment of a Black republic in 1791. The ability of slaves to overthrow and then run their own affairs must have inspired other slaves in Jamaica that they could do the same. For example, during her stay on the island from 1801 to 1807, as the wife of Governor General George, Lady Nugent records how the news of San Domingo was discussed over dinner and at regular gatherings of the island's elites. Furthermore, she concedes that by praising the strength, dignity and know-how of the slave leader Toussaint Louverture may have unwittingly encouraged the slaves in attendance. As she puts it, 'the blackies in attendance ... hardly changed a plate or do anything but listen'.[2]

Second is the belief that the abolition of the slave trade in 1807 meant that the abolition of slavery was imminent. In the first two decades of the nineteenth century, the island was awash with conspiracy theories based on the belief that Britain had granted freedom to slaves and that the island authorities were denying slaves their liberty. As one local magistrate put it, 'there is a general expectation among the Negroes, that of freedom being given shortly by the government'.[3] These theories were based, in part, on hearing of the abolition struggle in England and the resentment of the whites in the colonies towards the movement in Britain. The resentment on one occasion in the Jamaican Assembly in 1830 spilt over into a desire to advocate for succession to the United States. The slaves' overwhelming rejection of slavery's false consciousness, that is, a sense that they were really free or had no right to be enslaved, as we shall see later, was fully exploited by Sam Sharpe and his followers to nurture a revolutionary hope and armed insurrection.

Finally, the internal fact was that Jamaica was ripe for rebellion because of the conditions in the west of the island, where the revolt originated. The west of Jamaica was primed for an uprising. There were some 30 per cent of the colony's workforce based there, 106,000 out of a total workforce of 310,000. Around 20,000 to 40,000 were involved in the revolt, and among them were a range of urban and rural Blacks, coloured and free men and women. There was, as Edward Kamau Braithwaite states, a psycho-cultural preparation for revolution by the early nineteenth century. For instance, there were two prior conspiracies to overthrow the British in 1816 and 1823. Even Sharpe himself admitted that he was hoping to organize the rebellion for some time and had hatched a plan some years prior.

Sam Sharpe

I want to say something now about the originator of the rebellion and the course of action that was taken. The rebellion was led by Sam Sharpe. Sharpe was a household slave and deacon at the (Baptist missionary) Thomas Burchell's church. Like many of the revolt's leaders, he was part of the elite of the labour force, possessing as much authority as a slave was permitted. Historians obsess over two features of Sharpe's persona. The first was his intellectual prowess. From all accounts, Sharpe was an outstanding leader blessed with an infectious charisma that influenced everyone who came into contact with him. He was also a powerful and persuasive orator, as attested to by his fellow conspirator, Gardiner, who said that he was 'wrought up almost to a state of madness' when Sharpe spoke. Curiously, also of interest to historians are his striking physical features. He was by all accounts a handsome man, blessed with flawless complexion. The second obsession is intriguing. Why are his features important to historical reflections on his actions? Could only a handsome man lead a rebellion in nineteenth-century Jamaica? Or could it be simply that even historians fall into the trap of a bio-politics that fixates on the Black male body?

Sharpe campaigned actively for change. Under the cover of the Baptist Church, he was able to move from plantation to plantation and, under the cover of prayer meetings, 'holding secret intercourse with those slaves whose co-operation he wished to enlist'.[4] From the outset, Sharpe deployed a politics of rumour. According to sociologists of rumour (yes, they do exist), rumour is a signifier; it may not be factually true but points to a deeper reality or anxiety. In this case, the reality was the abhorrence of slavery, and, in response to this reality, Sharpe presented fiction as fact. Where the authorities were absent, he told congregations that slavery had been abolished and that the British were holding the slaves captive against their will. Where the authorities were present, Sharpe was more economical with the truth and said nothing about the alleged change in the law. However, rumour cannot be controlled, and neither can the actions that result. By using rumour, Sharpe was priming the people for radical action. He planned that they all agree to 'a set down after Christmas'. This would be a peaceful protest, and Sharpe said to his followers, 'We must not trouble anybody and raise no rebellion.' A point attested to by Baptist minister William Knibb in his testimony to parliament after the revolt was suppressed:

> There was no design of leaving the property, but they intended what would be called in England a turn out, till they were promised remuneration for their labour ...[5]

But Sharpe was a political realist and knew that if they were forced to go back to work, then they would have to resist with force. This is a curious position to hold. On the one hand, advocating passivity, but on the other, being armed and ready to propel any attack. It is a political perspective that has reson-ance in the history of the Black Atlantic raising its head in Black nationalist debates on the role of violence in the liberation struggle. Black theologian James Cone, reflecting on the ethics of violence, agrees that the default position of people of faith is non-violence but that in a world of violence, oppressed people should have the right to use violence, especially in self-defence.

By the evening of 28 December at 11 o'clock, the sky in the south-west was illuminated. Pandemonium reigned in Mon-tego Bay with rumours that rebel slaves were going to set the town ablaze. The authorities had not been caught unawares. Tensions were high well before the end of December as an incident at Salt Spring Estate earlier in the month had led the magistrates to order the commanding officer of the militia to send a company of the 22nd Regiment to the bay. Missionaries were also aware of the threat of revolt and urged patience. As late as 27 December, missionary William Knibb tried to persuade slaves at Moses Baker's Chapel that the rumours about freedom having been granted were false. But the rise in consciousness and heightened expectation was more powerful than the persuasive words of Knibb or even the fear of death.

The rebellion was a failure. Within a few months of fighting the small bands of courageous but ill-trained rebels, British troops and local militia were able to regain control of the western parishes, the epicentre of the dissent. But the ultimate goal of the rebels – Sharpe, Gardiner and others – was accomplished. The rebellion provided a final and decisive blow to the slave economy and was a spur for the abolitionists' great victory in 1834.

Given the significance of the rebellion in the Caribbean and British history, why do we in Britain know so little about Sam Sharpe and the slaves who ended slavery? For example, I was speaking to a colleague of mine, who is based in the history department, about this lecture today. I told him the topic of the lecture, and he replied that he knew the name (Sam Sharpe) but could not intellectually locate the history. My colleague is a young and gifted African-Caribbean scholar specializing in American presidents. If he is not aware of this history and its position in Caribbean and British history, what hope is there for others?

Why Do We Know So Little about Sam Sharpe?

Sam Sharpe is one of the least known or celebrated Jamaican national heroes among the Caribbean diaspora in Britain. There are no reggae songs dedicated to him, no dance hall moves or traditions of resistance named after him. What are the reasons for this lack of awareness and interest?

The first reason concerns historiography and is the result of colonial suppression. After the rebellion, the British colonial regime did all that they could to eradicate the memory of the Baptist War as an act of control. As Michel Foucault reminds us, history is always within power relationships, so that control of history facilitates control of the people. While post-independence Jamaica has made great efforts to insurrect the subjugated history of Sharpe, political suppression of Caribbean history remains a feature of the post-colonial domestic context of Britain, where Caribbean history is set in a marginal position in relation to the 'real' history of British monarchs, industrial development and wars. For instance, in my daughter's school in the Midlands, Black children explore one Caribbean figure only for a few minutes during the years they are present at primary school. I do not think that level of cultural literacy is good for Black, white or Asian children in a diverse nation or globalized economy.

The second reason is the change in the Black Christian demographic in the Caribbean and Britain. In the post-war period, the fastest-growing Christian denominations in both contexts were Pentecostal and evangelical groups. Neither tradition views the Baptist heritage as part of their theological formation. Further, these Christian traditions have tended to draw a dichotomy between theology and politics, and this perspective further discourages investigation and appreciation of the Baptist War.

The final reason for the lack of awareness is the increased distance between Jamaica and its diaspora in Britain. Time and space have weakened interest in Caribbean history and its implications for Britain's cosmopolitan culture. The historical void created by the vacation of Caribbean history is filled by African American history. At its best, African American history has raised awareness of Black history by providing intellectual resources and even a special month for remembering. But at its worst, African American history is hegemonic – it dominates Black history like an empire's reign over subjugated people. The results of this hegemony are stark. Young Black people in Britain, even those of Jamaican ancestry, are likely to know more about Harriet Tubman and Sojourner Truth than the slaves who abolished slavery in the Caribbean.

The Making and Re-making of Sam Sharpe

So, how do we revive this history, make it have an impact and relevance to diaspora subjects in Britain? Let us begin by looking at official and academic approaches before turning to the tactical approach. The official approach to reviving the history has been to work with anniversaries. Anniversaries have memorializing power, that is, the potential to make us remember in new ways – but only under certain conditions. Both 2012 and 2013 are important anniversaries in Jamaican history: 2012 is the fiftieth Anniversary of Jamaican independence from the British Empire, and 2013 is the one hundred and seventy-fifth anniversary of the abolition of the British plantation slavery in Jamaica and other British colonies in the Caribbean.

The official attempt to revive Sam Sharpe relates to the second anniversary of the abolition of slavery. The slave trade was abolished in 1807, and slavery in Britain's colonies in 1934/38. In Caribbean history, it is the slaves rather than the abolitionists who are foregrounded as those who ended slavery, and there is none greater in this pantheon of abolitionists than Sam Sharpe. However, memorialization is problematic. Anniversaries are problematic because they are often more celebratory than critical. A useful way of thinking about memory and transformation is through the work of political theologian Johann Metz.

In *The Emergent Church*, Metz reflects on memory, specifically the memory of the Holocaust.[6] He argues that the modern world is characterized by a loss of memory, particularly the memory of suffering. For Metz, historical memory has power, and its loss renders us less able to cope with the onslaught of 'marketplace' values and world views of the wider society. Loss of memory, or 'massive forgetfulness', paves the way for fatalism and apathy. In response, Metz calls for a new moral imagination that must ensure the 'memory of suffering accumulated in history'.[7] The memory of suffering has the potential to uncover falsehoods of evolutionary thinking by exposing the 'senseless suffering inflicted upon people in the name of human progress'. These 'dangerous memories' are

Memories, which make demands on us. There are memories in which earlier experiences break through to the centre point of our lives and reveal new and dangerous insights for the present. They illuminate for a few moments and with a harsh and steady light the questionable nature of things we have apparently come to terms with and show up the banality of our supposed 'realism'. Such memories are like dangerous and incalculable visitations from the past. They are memories that we have to take into account, memories, as it were, with a future content.[8]

Memorializing rarely makes the demands of dangerous memories. As Marx put it, once a revolutionary figure is appropriated by the state, they no longer have revolutionary power. A national hero, while an important historical memory, is, nonetheless, the state's construction of memory that reduces revolutionary potential into statues, textbooks and lecture series – hardly the stuff of revolution. Another way of reviving the history are the attempts by academics to revise the Baptist War. There are at least four types of revision at work. These are the cult of heroic genius, precursor, Black radicalism and the religious.

Cult of Heroic Genius

Heroic genius is the history of mostly the great Black men of the Caribbean. Heroic genius describes the innate ability of the individual – their talent to inspire others. Heroic genius may also include moral courage. Moral courage is a quality of character whereby an individual is willing to maintain their commitment to justice and what they know to be right despite personal danger, loss or the size and veracity of their opponents.

The heroic genius motif is a feature of Walter Rodney's impressive analysis of Caribbean traditions of resistance. Rodney weaves together a materialist and Black nationalist gaze on Caribbean history to produce a cryptic Black socialist historiography. Walter's history of the Caribbean reduces it to a Manichaean struggle between the European colonizers and slave masses. This conflict is set within a shifting economic climate that moves from mercantile to industrial capitalism from the seventeenth to the nineteenth century. This reading of class struggle in the Caribbean has little interest or appreciation of the abolitionist movement in England or the missionary class in the Caribbean. Both represent different strands of bourgeois capitalism. Furthermore, within this reading, Sam Sharpe is portrayed as a heroic leader and freedom fighter who leads the Black masses against the tyranny of the Jamaican plantocracy.

Heroic genius motifs in Black history live on the bright sight of human nature and ignore the grotesque. Indeed, one weakness of heroic genius is that it does not make space for what we can learn from the grotesque – and any meaningful history should consider both sides of human nature and behaviour. But the real issue here for me is that the heroic genius presupposes a masculinist biological determinism where heroes appear as ready-made Black men rather than complex everyday characters wrestling with the existential absurdity of being Black in a world of white supremacy.

Precursor

Another version of the Sharpe history is as a precursor to abolition. This approach is very popular with English historians of the Caribbean. The precursor reading views the Baptist War as the precursor to the main event, the parliament's abolition of slavery in 1834. It foregrounds the abolitions and only makes space for Jamaica and her brave slave army, at best, as a feature of the final push of parliamentary democracy for abolition and, at worst, on the margins of the modernist project to declare all men and women fully human. Also, within the precursor reading, Sharpe's rebellion is subtly contrasted with the events in parliament. Sharpe takes the form of a noble savage, a good-looking one, though, and the rebellion an orgy of violence. In contrast, the abolitionists are portrayed as persistent, moral and determined men and women who make use of parliamentary democracy rather than brute force.

The contradiction at the heart of the precursor tradition is that while seeking to include slave narratives in the story of abolition, it can only do so in a way that maintains a neo-colonial historiography that unwittingly reproduces an abolition racial hierarchy – ironically, a process that runs counter to the aims of the revolt itself.

Black Resistance

The next approach is resistance. Resistance interpretations make their starting point the distinction between opposition and resistance. *Opposition* denotes the challenge to a social system from within. It accepts a priori the basis on which the dominant group negotiates power and works with these tools to agitate for change. We may think of the Anti-Slavery Movement and, indeed, many of the Baptist missionaries to Jamaica in the first three decades of the nineteenth century as types of oppositional practice: the former working in parliament and the latter in the fields teaching slaves to read. In contrast, *resistance* takes place outside the system, making use of tools and practices also from outside the system. Resistance can be non-violent, as was the case with the so-called slave women's 'petticoat rebellion', and other ways of slowing down the mechanisms of slavery. Violent resistance is outright rebellion and armed insurrection, and it is the latter category into which falls the Baptist War.

Resistance readings of the Baptist War focus on the tools of resistance. For instance, Richard E. Burton's reading of the rebellion identifies the ideology, aesthetics and choreography of the Baptist War.

The *ideology* for the war was the Christian faith. Sharpe and his followers, from reading the Bible, came to the conclusion that no person had the right to enslave another. Furthermore, that it was better to die on the gallows than live a life of servitude. The *aesthetics* are registered in the overlap between the slave festivals and slave revolts. The titles that the militants gave each other (captain, general) and also the dress codes – dressing in military regalia similar to the blue jackets and black cross belts and red uniforms worn during John Cunoe (*Junkanoo*) and Christmas festivals. This rebellion aesthetic reveals a flow of resistance ideologies that bleed into each other. Finally, the *choreography* describes the tactics deployed by the leadership. On this matter, Burton is scathingly dismissive. Burton suggests that despite being prepared for protest, the leadership had no idea of what to do if their demands were granted or the war won. I will argue later that Burton's analysis does not ring true when we take a much closer look at the tactics of the rebellion.

Resistance motifs are under suspicion in the modern world. This is partly because of the loss of social movements in Black communities and the retreat into the self. As a result, resistance has become a matter of style, taste and aesthetics rather than a social ethic.

Religion

The final approach is religious. The religious history of rebellion is preoccupied with the role of Christian belief in shaping the dissent. After all, Sharpe was a Baptist, and the rebellion was known as the Baptist War. The Baptist tradition is unique in the Caribbean. Its origins lie with the missionary activity of freed African American slave George Liele in the late eighteenth century. As a Black missionary to Jamaica, Liele was better able to engage with the slave population and also synthesize African religious retentions with Christian thought and practice. Indeed, theologians suggest that the Baptist tradition reflects a religious adaptation of African religious traditions, including a commitment to freedom found in traditional African religion. Freedom was a feature of Sharpe's biblical hermeneutic. He believed that whites had no right to enslave Blacks, as Blacks had no right to enslave whites. Furthermore, that resistance to whites was justified in the eyes of God.

Religious readings, however, avoid the pressing question of the legitimacy of the Black violence at the heart of the protest. While there is much evidence to suggest that the original plan was a non-violent protest, the armed resistance that ensued was not completely accidental but instead a part of the plan.

In the modern world, Black violence as a legitimate response to racial terror is an anathema, possibly more so in Christian than secular contexts. According to African American Black theologian James Cone, Black Christian non-violence reflects an ideological negotiation that neglects the contestant and habitual violence of western states against their Black subjects. That is to say, by calling on all subjects and subjugated people to be non-violent while the state remains violent towards them. Thus, the rebellion raises the precarious question of who decides how the oppressed should go about the business of liberation. This is a question yet to be answered effectively by the religious rereadings of the history.

In sum, all of the interpretations of the Sharpe event have made an important contribution, but I believe that they fail to effectively revive the history so that it functions as a catalyst for change today, especially among the Jamaican diaspora in Britain. In response, I want to propose an alternative reading of Sharpe as a master tactician. A tactical reading of the rebellion does not seek to memorialize or essentialize Sharpe but instead to tease out instructions or rules for how we might address injustice today.

Tactician

I think that all of these interpretations, while important and defining approaches to the history, have failed to acknowledge a central motif running throughout the Sharpe event, that is, his tactical ability. At the heart of the rebellion was meticulous planning. Sharpe used the relative freedom he was granted as a slave preacher to organize bands of slaves on the west of the island. Prayer meetings become community organizing and sermons subversive counter-narrative. Community organizing is a good way of thinking about Sharpe's position or what Gramsci termed his 'war of maneuver',[9] and to this end, I want to use this theme as a way of reinterpreting the rebellion as the expression of radical tactics.

But we should ask the question – is it right to think of Sharpe in such modernist terms – as a community organizer? After all, projecting contemporary ideas backwards is always fraught with difficulty. This is because imposing contemporary standards on previous generations is problematic. But in reality, it is difficult, if not impossible, to avoid projecting back some sense of value, ethic or standard just by virtue of doing historical investigation. So, it might be best to think of reflecting back in terms of intellectual honesty. That is to say, the researcher needs to do their best to reflect critically on the reality of the historical context, the difficulties of applying any method and the tools deployed to unlock the situation.

With these limitations in mind, I want to make use of the work of the patriarch of community organizing, Saul David Alinsky, to reread Sam Sharpe as a master tactician. Saul Alinsky's ideas have experienced a recent revival due in part to the recovery of community organizing as a result of the rise of US President Barack Obama. Obama was a community organizer in Chicago before running for Senate and later becoming the first Black man of mixed parentage to become an American president. Alinsky's methods are greeted with as much scorn and praise by the opposing poles of American political life. For the right, he is an Anti-American communist sympathizer and agitator. For the left, he symbolizes the tactical arm that assisted aspects of the civil rights movement, union action and anti-poverty groups in the cauldron of 1960 politics in America. Whatever the position from which we may gaze on Alinsky, we cannot deny his enduring influence on urban American politics and the current US president (Barack Obama).

There is a natural resonance between Sam Sharpe's nineteenth-century Jamaican liberation movement and Saul Alinsky. Jamaican liberation involved organizing the Black proletariat against the colonial regime. Alinsky worked primarily but not exclusively in American ghettos in California, Michigan and New York City, organizing the Black poor against corporate greed and the apathy of the federal government in the 1950s. Both utilized Scriptures to justify their mission. For Sam Sharpe, it was the belief in the equality of all humanity, and for Alinsky it was biblical figures that function as models of action. Alinsky was able to codify his approach to resistance or community organizing within his 1970 publication *Rules for Radicals*. Rereading Sam Sharpe through the lens of Alinsky, I want to reveal how Sharpe exemplifies the community organizer and also identify some of Sharpe's rules for radicals and their importance today.

The Making of an Organizer

For Alinsky, organizing is the process of highlighting whatever he/she believes to be wrong and convincing people they can do something about it. The two are linked. If people feel they do not have the power to change a situation, they stop thinking about it. According to Alinsky, the organizer must first overcome suspicion and establish credibility. Next, the organizer must begin the task of agitating: rubbing resentments, fanning hostilities and searching out controversy. This is necessary to get people to participate. Alinsky would say, 'The first step in community organization is community disorganization.' Finally, through a process combining hope and resentment, the organizer tries to create a 'mass army' that brings in as many recruits as possible from local organizations, churches, service groups, labour unions, corner gangs and individuals.

Sharpe was an organizer. First, he had credibility. He was a Baptist minister, a respected orator, and not lacking in charisma. When he spoke, people listened. As an organizer, it was not difficult for him to convince others of their perilous predicament. After all, as I have suggested earlier, slavery in the Caribbean was occult practice. To fan the flames of discontent, Sharpe agitated for change. He made use of what sociologists term the politics of rumour. He spread the belief that the slaves had been made free in England and that the British in the colonies were resisting Black emancipation. We can only imagine how much this misinformation must have agitated slaves and placed them in opposition to both the state and the missionaries.

Finally, he created an army. As a Baptist minister, Sharpe

was given relatively free movement between plantations. He took this opportunity to organize slaves into a resistance movement in two ways. First, there was a division of labour. He modelled the military structure of the British army and gave his colleagues military titles such as general or corporal. Second, he had a plan. The idea was to refuse to work after the Christmas holiday of 1831 and negotiate a waged labour society where Blacks would be remunerated for their labour. Every effort was made to ensure that there would be a viable and intact social and economic fabric after the dispute. To this end, the warning signal for the protest was the lighting of trash houses where the waste product of the sugar refining was deposited. The trash houses had no value to the maintenance of the mechanism of production.

Sam Sharpe's *Rules for Radicals*

Alinsky also identified rules for radicals – how they were to engage with the powers that be in order to effect change. For instance, Rule 3: 'Whenever possible, go outside the expertise of the enemy.' Look for ways to increase insecurity, anxiety and uncertainty. And Rule 4: 'Make the enemy live up to its own book of rules.'[10] But Sharpe had his own rules, and in closing I want to identify three.

He learned to read

Reading in colonial Jamaica was almost exclusive to the colonial regime and the few free Blacks and coloureds who were able to secure tuition, usually from the religious authorities, particularly the Methodist and Baptist missions. Teaching slaves to read was a subversive act because slavery's structure depended upon solipsism – the institutionalization of ignorance – for its maintenance. However, the missionaries realized that every literate slave was a potential obstacle in the way of slavery's mystification and obfuscation of facts. Literacy was, therefore, more than education; it was also a theo-political act born of a subversive imagination. Reading gave Sharpe access to books and newspapers – the internet of the first worldwide industrial revolution. He consumed every aspect of the abolition discussion occurring in Britain and came to the conclusion that the abolition of slavery in England in 1826 was de facto freedom for slaves in the English colonies. He was legally wrong but theologically right. Education matters in the Caribbean diaspora in Britain also. I do not want to rehearse the facts and figures here but only to say that when you incarcerate more Black men than we send to university, education becomes a civil rights issue. So, rule number 1: knowledge is power; know the facts behind your predicament.

He constructed an ideology

Sharpe's ideology proclaimed the equality of all people and also the right to struggle for justice. What we might term today 'no justice, no peace'. Equality was based on religious grounds. After all, religion set the moral standard and was the basis of the slave's appeal for freedom from the beginning of the slave trade. Colonial Christian religion, however, was contradictory, and Sharpe understood this but seized upon the truth of freedom in Christ as the basis for a freedom for all.

His simple interpretation of the text was a counter to the supremacist ideology of whiteness and the theology of Empire. Whiteness, the social superiority of the British Empire, was based on Black subjugation and justified this view with pseudoscience and biblical misinterpretation. The theology of Empire also placed human progress and industry at the centre of its reason for being. Economic development and the destruction of encountered peoples in the New World were all part of its metaphysic. That is, the newly encountered peoples of the New World and African slaves were not fully human and, therefore, expendable. Sharpe's reasoning challenges both. Divine justice and equity had to replace whiteness and the religious logic of Empire as signs of real progress and development. In sum,

Sharpe developed a political theology as ideology: one where the people of God stand against hierarchy and power and the political economy that ravages the poor.

Legitimacy of protest

Finally, Sharpe possessed what most Black Christians today have neglected – the ability and desire to protest. Historians have spent a great deal of time and energy trying to work out whether the protest was intentionally violent. But this perspective misses the point. The point for Sharpe was that protest is not only a legitimate practice in the face of oppression but also a fundamental tactic for social transformation. No protest, no change.

In Conclusion

The history of Sam Sharpe is hotly contested. While traditional readings have focused on the individual heroic genius, radical perspectives have augmented his revolutionary intent. While both have their place in the politics of remembering, I believe that a strategist reading is the most potent way of remembering for contemporary Britain. A strategist approach forces us to apply several principles of community organizing, such as causing agitation, engaging with the real needs of people – their self-interests – and also actively participating in processes of change.

Sam Sharpe stands tall among Jamaican heroes but will never receive the honour that his legacy deserves unless we as individuals and groups decide to each become Sam Sharpe, which is to organize for change and not opt out of the struggle – that is, 'deliver us from evil'.

Notes

1 Alinsky, Saul D. (1971), *Rules for Radicals: A Practical Primer for Realistic Radicals*, New York: Random House.

2 Bohls, Elizabeth A. (2014), *Slavery and the Politics of Place: Representing the Colonial Caribbean, 1770–1833*, Cambridge: Cambridge University Press.

3 Ogborn, Miles (2019), *The Freedom of Speech: Talk and Slavery in the Anglo-Caribbean World*, Chicago: University of Chicago Press.

4 Bleby, Henry (1853), *Death Struggles of Slavery: Being a narrative of facts and incidents, which occurred in a British colony, during the two years immediately preceding negro emancipation*, London: Hamilton, Adams.

5 House of Commons (1833), *Report from the Select Committee on the Extinction of Slavery Throughout the British Dominions*, London: J. Haddon.

6 Metz, Johann Baptist (1981), *The Emergent Church: The Future of Christianity in a Postbourgeois World*, London: SCM Press.

7 Metz, *The Emergent Church*.

8 Metz, *The Emergent Church*.

9 Gramsci, Antonio (1971), *Selections from the Prison Notebooks of Antonio Gramsci*, ed. and trans. Quintin Hoare and Geoffrey Nowell Smith, New York: International Publishers.

10 Alinsky, *Rules for Radicals*.

Editor's Reflections:
Strategies for a New Decade

Dr E. P. Louis

It has been my honour to bring together such incredible lectures on the legacy of Sam Sharpe from the last decade. The Sam Sharpe Project is driven to pursue justice in the form of reparations, and each of these lectures, in their own way, demonstrates the necessity for reparation and for Christians to be behind this biblical mechanism.

My journey with the Sam Sharpe Project has been that of the intern, surrounded by accomplished, experienced and convicted elders who have committed themselves to challenge colonial Christianity and to uncover biblical truths that speak against racialized injustices that, have affected our ancestors – those Africans sold and exchanged in the slave trade centuries ago, their children who endured bondage and horrific, deviant and nearly unforgivable treatment (but for Christ). We are of the opinion, to varying degrees, that the legacy of those horrors still affects Black and Brown people's ability to flourish in today's global society and therefore turn to a biblical premise for *reparation.*

It has been incredible to watch Rosemarie Davidson and Revd Wale Hudson-Roberts work with their networks, supporters, allies and colleagues each year, resulting in annual lectures and, more recently, webinars that speak with wisdom, valour and courage from the past to the concerns of today. In the Foreword, we see a bit about Rosemarie's high and lofty vision for the Sam Sharpe Lectures (rightly so!), and her gratitude to all those who have made a significant contribution to the life of the Sam Sharpe Lectures through funding, goodwill, reparatively and in partnership, but there is also something to be said for the way they encourage those of us coming up. Revd Wale, through the Sam Sharpe Project, has provided many opportunities for my professional development. However, most importantly, he has created a safe and encouraging space in which I and others, over time, can figure out how we can be a Sam Sharpe in today's society, how all of us can figure out the shape and scope of our contribution – how our theology and raw conviction of the gospel informs the outworking of our service as God's servants to the world, despite the colonial perversion of servanthood. Wale, like Sam Sharpe, is very much the organizer – so much vision and so many emails!

Rosemarie and Wale have created an important space for peers collectively to organize ourselves for the immense task of teaching, facilitating and realizing justice for our people worldwide. While all of our contributors have been creating incredible legacies of their own, it is great to see how they work together in book form through this collection of thinking, theologizing and organizing. These are not merely deep dives into history but instructive of the next steps: standing upon the foundations laid for the last few centuries by our ancestors.

I hope that when you have been reading, you have been able to *hear* the lectures; I have done my best to try and maintain the *oral*-ness of each lecture rather than turn them into essays because, while written documentation is important, oral transmissions carry so much depth and texture that it provides a multidimensional experience with the speaker's ideas, background, epistemological framework and personality.[1] As you tackle each lecture, I hope that the resulting non-uniformity makes for dynamic reading. I have two very brief thoughts out of the many things that have impacted me while bringing together these lectures. The first is about 'our position', and the second is about how we identify Christianity.

Our Position

Kehinde's existential crisis is undeniably felt by many Black and Brown people in the first world who are experiencing privileges, luxury and comfort that many of our people around the world do not have access to. Apart from ancestry, racism and discrimination can often be our only shared experience – for some, it means unemployment, and for others it means starvation or death. What Sam Sharpe shows us and what Kehinde elaborates on is that every position can have a purposeful and meaningful part to play in enacting, facilitating or demanding justice. Most notable is how uncomfortable it will be – comfort (for those of us in Britain) is our enemy while in this battle against sin; for all of us of all ethnicities, discomfort and confrontation is the slave-preacher and repenters portion. This is not dissimilar to what we see in the ministry and teaching of Yeshua (Christ):

> If the world hates you, know that it has hated me before it hated you. If you were of the world, the world would love you as its own; but because you are not of the world, but I chose you out of the world, therefore the world hates you. Remember the word that I said to you: 'A servant is not greater than his master.' If they persecuted me, they will also persecute you. If they kept my word, they will also keep yours. But all these things they will do to you on account of my name, because they do not know him who sent me. If I had not come and spoken to them, they would not have been guilty of sin, but now they have no excuse for their sin. Whoever hates me hates my Father also. If I had not done among them the works that no one else did, they would not be guilty of sin, but now they have seen and hated both me and my Father. (John 15.18–24)

This is not to confuse the hate the people of colour receive with the hate that Christians who preach the gospel, seeking justice and bringing light to the darkness of injustice, receive. Many of us are both Christians and people of colour and so experience the double portion of hate and discomfort, and while both these forms of hate are born of humanity's inequity, Christ has never taught that people of colour are expected to be hated for the way that they look and where they come from. The hate Christ speaks about, the discomfort we experience in our various positions as his children and as agents of justice, signifies our effectiveness in talking truth to power. No matter what role we may occupy, so far as you are employed by the world, your comfort, longevity and security are not to be taken for granted.

Humanity is Not the Standard of Christianity

When we talk about the era of the physical mass African enslavement and colonization by the Europeans and the complicity of European churches, I am reminded that if we claim that Christ is the standard of righteousness, justice, love, mercy and forgiveness, then we must maintain our distinction of the colonial church and not conflate it with biblical Christianity and/or the body of Christ. Surely, if we can condemn the historical churches' involvement and justification, then we are condemning the religion they have relied upon to support their claims of superiority. If we continue to say 'the church' or Christians, in these broad terms for European religious enslavers, slave-owners and colonial Christianizers, then are we not, in turn, condemning Christ, the author and finisher of our faith? Moreover, how can we then help people to see that in repentance, in turning away from the sin of racism and colonialism, they are leaving one perverse pseudo-religion for the religion of the Bible (or Christian faith) as led and taught by the Son of God?

Further to this, as we reflect on the terror of the colonial church on Black and Brown bodies and white minds, there were other bodies of Christians around the world, in the Afroasiatic region particularly, who are not part of this 'church'. I am reminded by and excited by the unfolding career of Dr Vince Bantu as he seriously engages the Ethiopian Orthodox Church as an alternative historical, theological and epistemological stream to the usual Rome-to-reform route many of us encounter in Christian educational institutions. Although not the first to make these considerations, as emerging Black Christian scholarship responds to the exodus of many young Black people from the mainstream church (on account of the legacy of slavery and colonialism) to alternative Black religious spaces, it is encouraging to see titles such as *Gospel Hymanot*[2] and *A Multitude of All Peoples: Engaging Ancient Christianity's Global Identity*[3] bridge the gap between an apologetic and emancipatory theological response to the evil of colonial Christianity.

Christ is the standard of our church, and what we can see in this collection of lectures is the burning desire of people like Sam Sharpe to correct this falsehood to the point of violence and death – over his dead body would people be allowed to accept colonial Christianity as a representation of Christ and his body. His insurrection and death are a witness to the truth, a witness to the Scriptures and to the unrivalled person of Christ, such as we see in Isaiah 61:

> The Spirit of the Lord GOD is upon me;
> because the LORD has anointed me
> to bring good news to the poor;
> he has sent me to bind up the brokenhearted,
> to proclaim liberty to the captives,
> and the opening of the prison to those who are bound;
> to proclaim the year of the LORD's favor,
> and the day of vengeance of our God;
> to comfort all who mourn;
> to grant to those who mourn in Zion –
> to give them a beautiful headdress instead of ashes,
> the oil of gladness instead of mourning,
> the garment of praise instead of a faint spirit;
> that they may be called oaks of righteousness,
> the planting of the LORD, that he may be glorified.
> They shall build up the ancient ruins;
> they shall raise up the former devastations;
> they shall repair the ruined cities,
> the devastations of many generations. (Isa. 61.1–4)

Sam Sharpe's legacy bears witness to this scripture's revelation – of the sacrifice, resurrection and return of Christ the Conqueror, the Lion of the Tribe of Judah. Christ is the standard. Sam Sharpe is a witness, a course-corrector in word and deed. This collection of lectures makes no mild calling, for 'History is a cyclical story of renewal, apostasy, repentance and redemption' (Revd Joel Edwards, Chapter 7), and so the work continues until His return.

Notes

1 My decision here I feel is further supported by some of Kehinde Andrews's notions in Chapter 1.

2 Bantu, Vince L. (2020), *Gospel Haymanot: A Constructive Theology and Critical Reflection on African and Diasporic Christianity*, Chicago, IL: Urban Ministries Inc.

3 Bantu, Vince (2020), *A Multitude of All Peoples: Engaging Ancient Christianity's Global Identity*, Westmont, IL: InterVarsity Press.

Bibliography

Ahmad A. and Wilkie, A. S. (1979), 'Technology Transfer in the New International Economic Order: Options, Obstacles, and Dilemmas', in J. McIntyre and D. S. Papp (eds), *The Political Economy of International Technology Transfer*, New York: Quorum Books.

Andrews, Kehinde (2013), *Resisting Racism: Race, Inequality, and the Black Supplementary School Movement*, London: Trentham Books Ltd.

Andrews, Kehinde (2019), *Back to Black: Retelling Black Radicalism for the 21st Century*, London: Bloomsbury Publishing.

Bailey, Anne C. (2006), *African Voices of the Transatlantic Slave Trade: Beyond the Silence and the Shame*, Boston: Beacon Press.

Beckles, Hilary (1999), *Centering Woman: Gender Discourses in Caribbean Slave Society*, Kingston: Ian Randle Publishers.

Beckles, Hilary McDonald (2016), *The First Black Slave Society: Britain's 'Barbarity Time' in Barbados, 1636–1876*, Mona: University of the West Indies Press.

Beckles, Hilary and Shepherd, Verene (2007), *Trading Souls: Europe's Transatlantic Trade in Africans, A Bicentennial Caribbean Reflection*, Kingston: Ian Randle Publishers.

Bennett Jr, J. Henry (1958), *Bondsmen and Bishops Slavery and Apprenticeship on Codrington Plantations in Barbados, 1710–1838*, Los Angeles: University of California Press.

Bleby, Henry (1853), *Death Struggles of Slavery: Being a Narrative of Facts and Incidents, Which Occurred in a British Colony, During the Two Years Immediately Preceding Negro Emancipation*, London: Hamilton, Adams.

Bohls, Elizabeth A. (2014), *Slavery and the Politics of Place: Representing the Colonial Caribbean, 1770–1833*, Cambridge: Cambridge University Press.

Braithwaite, Lloyd (2001), *Colonial West Indian Students in Britain*, Mona: University of the West Indies Press.

Brathwaite, Kamau (1971), *Development of Creole Society in Jamaica, 1770–1820*, Kingston: Ian Randle Publishers.

Bronowski, Jacob (2011), *The Ascent Of Man*, London: BBC Books.

Callam, Neville (1998), 'Hope: A Caribbean Perspective', *Ecumenical Review* 50(2), April, pp. 137–42.

Campbell, John (1951), *Negromania: Being an Examination of the Falsely Assumed Equality of the Various Races of Men*, Philadelphia: Campbell and Power.

Carlyle, Thomas (1888), *Thomas Carlyle's Works: Critical and Miscellaneous Essays*, vols 1–3, London: Chapman and Hall.

Carmichael, S. (Kwame Ture) (2007), *Stokely Speaks: From Black Power to Pan-Africanism*, 1st edn, Chicago: Review Press.

Carter, Kameron J. (2008), *Race: A Theological Account*, Oxford: Oxford University Press.

Conford, Revd P. H. (1895), *Missionary Reminiscences or Jamaica Retraced*, Leeds: J. Heaton & Son.

Costas, Orlando (2005), *Christ Outside the Gate: Mission Beyond Christendom*, Oregon: Wipf and Stock.

Cox, Edward (1984), *Free Coloureds in the Slave Societies of St Kitts and Grenada*, Knoxville: University of Tennessee Press.

Cranston, Maurice (1999), *The Noble Savage: Jean-Jacques Rousseau, 1754–1762*.

Dadzie, Stella (2020), *A Kick in the Belly*, London: Verso Press.

Davis, Carole Boyce (2010), *Claudia Jones: Beyond Containment*, Banbury: Ayebia Clarke Publishing.

Davis, David Brian (1970), *The Problem of Slavery in Western Culture*, New York: Cornell University Press.

De Gruchy, John (2005), *Daring, Trusting Spirit: Bonhoeffer's Friend Eberhard Bethge*, Minneapolis: Fortress Press.

Dick, Devon (2002), *Rebellion to Riot, The Jamaican Church in Nation Building*, Kingston: Ian Randle Publishers.

Dick, Devon (2009), *The Cross and Machete: Native Baptists of Jamaica*, Kingston: Ian Randle Publishers.

Dick, Devon (2012), 'Lessons from Sam Sharpe', *Gleaner*, 24 May.

Drescher, Seymour (1982), *Capitalism and Anti-Slavery*, New York: Macmillan Press.

DuBois, William E. B. (1964), *The World and Africa*, New York: International Publishers.

Dunn, Hopeton (ed.) (2007), *Emancipation: The Lessons and the Legacy*, Kingston: Arawak Publications.

Eliav-Feldon, Isaac, Miriam Benjamin and Ziegler, Joseph (eds) (2009), *Origins of Racism in the West*, Cambridge: Cambridge University Press.

Erskine, Noel (1981), *Decolonizing Theology: A Caribbean Perspective*, Maryknoll: Orbis Books.

Euripides (1891), *The Plays of Euripides*, trans. E. P. Coleridge, Vol. II, London: George Bell and Sons. Available at: http://www.perseus.tufts.edu/hopper/text?doc=Perseus%3Atext%3A1999.01.0108%3Acard%3D1374 (accessed 30.6.23).

Fausto Vasconcelos (ed.) (2011), *Baptist Faith and Witness, Book 4*, Falls Church: Baptist World Alliance.

BIBLIOGRAPHY

Ferguson, Niall (2003), *Empire: The Rise and Demise of the British World Order and the Lessons for Global Power*, New York: Basic Books.

Ferguson, Niall (2012), *Civilization: The West and the Rest*, London: Penguin Books.

Fischer, Sibylle (2004), *Modernity Disavowed: Haiti and the Cultures of Slavery in the Age of Revolution*, Durham, NC, and London: Duke University Press.

Flynn, James (1980), *Race, IQ and Jansen*, London: Routledge & Kegan Paul.

Goodall, Norman (ed.) (1968), *The Uppsala Report 1968: Official Report of the Fourth Assembly of the World Council of Churches, Uppsala, July 4–20, 1968*, Geneva: WCC.

Gonzalez, Justo L. (2014), *The Story of Christianity: The Early Church to the Dawn of the Reformation*, vol. 1, New York: HarperOne.

Goveia, Elsa (1965), *Slave Society in the British Leeward Islands*, New Haven: Yale University Press.

Green, T. and Grose, T. (eds) (1886), 'Of National Characters', in *The Philosophical Works of David Hume*, vol. 3, London: Longmans.

Hall, Catherine, Draper, Nicholas, et al. (2014), *Legacies of British Slave-ownership: Colonial Slavery and the Formation of Victorian Britain*, Cambridge: Cambridge University Press.

Hall, Douglas (1989), *In Miserable Slavery: Thomas Thistlewood in Jamaica, 1750–1786*, London: Macmillan.

Hannaford, Ivan (1996), *Race: The History of an Idea in the West*, Washington, DC: The Woodrow Wilson Press.

Higman, Barry (1995), *Slave Population and Economy in Jamaica, 1807–1834*, Barbados, Jamaica, Trinidad & Tobago: The University Press.

Hirschman, Charles (2004), 'The Origins and Demise of the Conception of Race', *Population and Development Review* 30(2), p. 401.

Hobson, Theo (2017), *God Created Humanism: The Christian Basis of Secular Values*, London: SPCK.

Hopkins, Dwight (2005), *Being Human: Race, Culture, and Religion*, Minneapolis: Fortress Press.

Hopkins, Dwight (2000), *Down, Up and Over: Slave Religion and Black Theology*, Minneapolis: Fortress Press.

Horton, James O. and Horton, Lois E. (eds) (2006), *Slavery and Public History: The Tough Stuff of American Memory*, New York: The New Press.

Howse, Ernest Marshall (1971), *Saints in Politics: The 'Clapham Sect' and the Growth of Freedom*, London: Allen and Unwin.

Howse, Ernest Marshall (2004), *Who Are We: The Challenge to America's National Identity*, New York: Simon and Schuster.

Huntington, Samuel P. (1996), *Clash of Civilizations and the Remaking of World Order*, London: Simon and Schuster.

Jakobsson, Stiv (1972), *Am I Not a Man and a Brother? British Missions and the Abolition of the Slave Trade and Slavery in West Africa and the West Indies 1786–1838*, Uppsala: Gleerup.

James, C. L. R. (1938/2001), *The Black Jacobins: Toussaint L'ouverture and the San Domingo Revolution*, London: Penguin Books.

James, Marlon (2010), *The Book of Night Women*, New York: Riverhead.

Jennings, Willie (2010), *The Christian Imagination: Theology and the Origins of Race*, New Haven & London: Yale University Press.

Kennedy, Fred (2008), *Daddy Sharpe: A Narrative of the Life and Adventures of Samuel Sharpe, a West Indian Slave, Written by Himself, 1832*, Kingston: Ian Randle Publishers.

Knox, Robert (1850), *The Races of Man: A Fragment*, Philadelphia: Lea & Blanchard.

Lauren, Paul Gordon (1988), *Power and Prejudice: The Politics and Diplomacy of Racial Discrimination*, Boulder: Westview.

Lawson, Winston (1996), *Religion and Race: African and European Roots in Conflict, A Jamaican Testament*, New York: Peter Lang.

Lewis, Gordon K. (2004), *The Growth of the Modern West Indies*, Kingston: Ian Randle Publishers.

Mair, Lucille Mathurin (2007), *A Historical Study of Women in Jamaica, 1655–1838*, Kingston: University of the West Indies Press.

Maldonaldo-Torres, N. 'On the Coloniality of Being', *Cultural Studies* 21(2), pp. 240–70. To link to this article: DOI: 10.1080/0950238060 1162548.

Marley, Bob and the Wailers (1973), *Slave Driver*, Tuff Gong & Island Records.

Marti, Jose (1975), *Inside the Monster: Writings on the United States and American Imperialism*, ed. Philip S. Foner, trans. Elinor Randall, New York: Monthly Review Press.

McIntyre, J. and Papp, D. S. (eds) (1979), *The Political Economy of International Technology Transfer*, New York: Quorum.

Metz, Johann Baptist (1981), *The Emergent Church: The Future of Christianity in a Postbourgeois World*, London: SCM Press.

Miller, David (1928), *The Drafting of the Covenant*, New York: Putnam.

Mills, Charles (1997), *The Racial Contract*, Ithaca: Cornell University Press.

Moltmann, Jürgen (1975), *The Church in the Power of the Holy Spirit: A Contribution to the Messianic Ecclesiology*, San Francisco: HarperCollins.

Moltmann, Jürgen (2010), *Theology of Hope*, trans. James W. Leitch, London: SCM Press.

Muir, Dr R. David (2014), *Slavery, Abolition and Diasporan Memory*

& the Curious Invisibility of Sam Sharpe from Baptist Centenary Historiography, a discussion paper, Regent's Park College, Oxford.

Mukwashi, Amanda Khozi (2020), *But Where Are You Really From?* London: SPCK.

Nicholson, Harold (1933), *Peacemaking, 1919*, Boston: Houghton Mifflin Company.

Ogborn, Miles (2019), *The Freedom of Speech: Talk and Slavery in the Anglo-Caribbean World*, Chicago: University of Chicago Press.

Paine, Thomas (1999), *The Rights of Man*, New York: Dover Publications.

Pakenham, Thomas (2015), *The Scramble for Africa*, London: Little, Brown Book Group.

Parrillo, Vincent (2002), *Understanding Race and Ethnic Relations*, Boston: Allyn and Bacon.

Patterson, Orlando (1982), *Slavery and Social Death: A Comparative Study*, Cambridge, MA, and London: Harvard University Press.

Priest, Robert and Nieves, Alvaro (eds) (2007), *This Side of Heaven: Race, Ethnicity, and Christian Faith*, New York: Oxford University Press.

Rankine, Claudia (2015), *Citizen*, London: Penguin Books.

Reddie, Anthony (ed.) (2010), *Black Theology, Slavery and Contemporary Christianity*, Surrey and Vermont: Ashgate Publishing Co.

Reid, C. S. (1988), *Samuel Sharpe: From Slave to National Hero*, Kingston: Bustamante Institute of Public Affairs.

Reid-Salmon, Delroy A. (2012), *Burning for Freedom: A Theology of the Black Atlantic Struggle for Liberation*, Kingston: Ian Randle Publishers.

Roberts, J. Deotis (2005), *Bonhoeffer and King: Speaking Truth to Power*, Louisville: Westminster John Knox Press.

Roberts, J. M. (2001), *The Triumph of the West*, London: Phoenix Press.

Robinson, Randall (2000), *The Debt: What America Owes the Blacks*, London: Penguin Books.

Rogers, Charles (ed.) (1876), *Boswelliana: The Commonplace Book of J. Boswell, with a Memoir and Annotations*, London: The Grampian Club.

Rousseau, Jean-Jacques (2017), *The Social Contract*, London: Arcturus Publishing.

Seely, Bruce (2003), 'Historical Patterns in the Scholarship of Technology Transfer', *Comparative Technology Transfer & Society* 1, April, pp. 7–48.

Senior, Bernard (1835), *Jamaica As It Is, As It Was and As It May Be*, London: T. Hurst.

Settles, Joshua Dwayne (1996), 'The Impact of Colonialism on African Economic Development', Chancellor's Honors Program Projects, https://trace.tennessee.edu/utk_chanhonoproj/182 (accessed 26.5.23).

Shepherd, Verene (2007), '"Petticoat Rebellion"?: Women in Emancipation', in *Emancipation: The Lessons and the Legacy*, ed. Hopeton Dunn, Kingston: Arawak Publications.

Shepherd, Verene (2009), *Livestock, Sugar and Slavery: Contested Terrain in Colonial Jamaica*, Kingston: Ian Randle Publishers.

Sherlock, Sir Phillip Manderson and Bennett, Hazel (1998), *The Story of the Jamaican People*, Kingston: Ian Randle Publishers.

Snelgrave, William (1754), *A New Account of Some Parts of Guinea and the Slave Trade*, London: James, John and Paul Knapton.

Spencer, Nick (2006), *Doing God*, London: Theos.

Sweet, James (1997), 'The Iberian Roots of Racist Thought', *William and Mary Quarterly*, LIV(1), January, pp. 143–66.

Trepagnier, Barbara (2010), *Silent Racism: How Well-Meaning White People Perpetuate the Racial Divide*, expanded edn, Boulder: Paradigm Publishers.

Whalin, W. Terry (1997), *Sojourner Truth: American Abolitionist*, Ohio: Barbour Publishing Inc.

William, St Clair (2007), *The Door of No Return: The History of the Cape Coast Castle and the Atlantic Slave Trade*, New York: Blue-Bridge.

Williams, Delores S. (1993), *Sisters in the Wilderness: The Challenge of Womanist God-talk*, Maryknoll: Orbis Books.

Williams, Eric (1984), *From Columbus to Castro: The History of the Caribbean 1492–1969*, New York City: Vintage Books.

Williams, Eric (1994), *Capitalism and Slavery*, Chapel Hill: University of North Carolina Press.

Wilmore, Gayraud S. (1986), *Black Religion and Black Radicalism: An Interpretation of the Religious History of Afro-American People*, Maryknoll: Orbis Books.

Winstedt, E. O. Cicero (trans.) (1918), *Letters to Atticus with an English, MA, of Magdalen College, Oxford*, London: William Heinemann Ltd & Cambridge, MA: Harvard University Press.

Wood, Marcus (ed.) (2003), *The Poetry of Slavery: An Anglo-American Anthology, 1764–1865*, Oxford: Oxford University Press.

Websites and Statements

American Anthropological Association Statement on Race. Available at: https://americananthro.org/about/policies/statement-on-race/ (accessed 30.6.23).

Anti-Slavery Monthly Reporter, Vol. IV, No. 77, 1 March 1831.

Boeskool, Chris, 'When you're accustomed to privilege and equality feels like oppression' (blog). Available at: https://www.huffpost.com/entry/when-youre-accustomed-to-privilege_b_9460662 (accessed 15.6.23).

Butschar to Nyländer (1809), extract, 16 September; from Klein to Pratt, 21 July, in Proceedings of CMS, 1812.

CARICOM Ten Point Plan for reparatory justice. Available at: https://caricom.org/caricom-ten-point-plan-for-reparatory-justice/ (accessed 30.6.23).

Coates, Ta-Nehisi (2015), 'Hope and the Historian', The Atlantic, 10 December. Available at: https://www.theatlantic.com/politics/archive/2015/12/hope-and-the-historian/419961/ (accessed 15.6.23).

Clarke, John (1850), 'Memoire of the Late Rev. Joseph Merrick', The Baptist Magazine 5.8, April, pp. 197–204. Available at: https://biblicalstudies.gospelstudies.org.uk/articles_baptist-magazine_03.php (accessed 30.6.23).

Declaration on Race and Racial Prejudice (1978). Available at: https://en.unesco.org/about-us/legal-affairs/declaration-race-and-racial-prejudice (accessed 15.6.23).

Durban Declaration and Programme of Action (2002), United Nations Department of Public Information New York. Available at: https://www.ohchr.org/sites/default/files/Documents/Publications/Durban_text_en.pdf (accessed 30.6.23).

House of Commons (1833), 'The Evidence of William Knibb', in Report from the Select Committee on the Extinction of Slavery Throughout the British Dominions, London: J. Haddon.

King Jr, Martin Luther (1967), 'A Time to Break Silence', Speech at Riverside Church, New York.

Rankine, Claudia (interview). Available at: https://www.theguardian.com/books/2015/dec/27/claudia-rankine-poet-citizen-american-lyric-feature (accessed 15.6.23).

Republic of South Africa (1996), 'Draft White Paper for Social Welfare', Government Gazette, Vol. 368, No. 16943, 2 February, p. 18. Available at: https://gazettes.africa/akn/za/officialGazette/government-gazette/1996-02-02/16943/eng@1996-02-02 (accessed 30.6.23).

Treaties and International Agreements Filed and Recorded from 20 March 1953 to 31 March 1953, United Nations Treaty Series (in English and French), Vol. 162, pp. 205–311.

UNESCO (1969), Four Statements on the Race Question. Available at: http://unesdoc.unesco.org/images/0012/001229/122962eo.pdf (accessed 15.6.23).

United Nations (2002), Human Rights: A Compilation of International Instruments of the United Nations. Available at: https://www.ohchr.org/sites/default/files/Documents/Publications/Compilation1en.pdf (accessed 30.6.23).

Watkins, Kevin (2021), 'Ending the "Trickle Down" vaccine Economics' (blog). Available at: https://www.project-syndicate.org/commentary/ending-trickle-down-vaccine-economics-by-kevin-watkins-2021-09 (accessed 15.6.23).

Index of Names and Subjects

Index of Bible References